Cambridge Elements ☰

Elements in Philosophy of Science
edited by
Jacob Stegenga
University of Cambridge

LOGICAL EMPIRICISM AS SCIENTIFIC PHILOSOPHY

Alan W. Richardson
University of British Columbia

CAMBRIDGE
UNIVERSITY PRESS

CAMBRIDGE
UNIVERSITY PRESS

Shaftesbury Road, Cambridge CB2 8EA, United Kingdom

One Liberty Plaza, 20th Floor, New York, NY 10006, USA

477 Williamstown Road, Port Melbourne, VIC 3207, Australia

314–321, 3rd Floor, Plot 3, Splendor Forum, Jasola District Centre,
New Delhi – 110025, India

103 Penang Road, #05–06/07, Visioncrest Commercial, Singapore 238467

Cambridge University Press is part of Cambridge University Press & Assessment,
a department of the University of Cambridge.

We share the University's mission to contribute to society through the pursuit of
education, learning and research at the highest international levels of excellence.

www.cambridge.org
Information on this title: www.cambridge.org/9781009471510

DOI: 10.1017/9781009471497

First published 2023

A catalogue record for this publication is available from the British Library

ISBN 978-1-009-47151-0 Hardback
ISBN 978-1-009-47147-3 Paperback
ISSN 2517-7273 (online)
ISSN 2517-7265 (print)

Logical Empiricism As Scientific Philosophy

Elements in Philosophy of Science

DOI: 10.1017/9781009471497
First published online: December 2023

Alan W. Richardson
University of British Columbia

Author for correspondence: Alan W. Richardson, Alan.richardson@ubc.ca

Abstract: This Element offers a new account of the philosophical significance of logical empiricism that relies on the past forty years of literature reassessing the project. It argues that while logical empiricism was committed to empiricism and did become tied to the trajectory of analytic philosophy, neither empiricism nor logical analysis per se was the deepest philosophical commitment of logical empiricism. That commitment was, rather, securing the scientific status of philosophy, bringing philosophy into a scientific conception of the world.

Keywords: analytic philosophy, empiricism, history of philosophy of science, logical empiricism, scientific philosophy

ISBNs: 9781009471510 (HB), 9781009471473 (PB), 9781009471497 (OC)
ISSNs: 2517-7273 (online), 2517-7265 (print)

Contents

Logical Empiricism: Reframing Its Philosophical
Significance   1

Logical Empiricism As Scientific Philosophy: Evidence
and Background   21

Logical Empiricist Scientific Philosophy: Consequences
and Legacies   45

References   65

Logical Empiricism: Reframing Its Philosophical Significance

Logical empiricism was one of the central projects in academic philosophy from roughly the late 1920s to the 1960s. It began in Europe, most importantly in Vienna and Berlin, and, with the rise of fascism in Europe, eventually reached its mature and most influential state in the United States of America. The first of the logical empiricists to emigrate from Europe to the United States was Herbert Feigl in 1931; he was followed in the 1930s by many others, including Gustav Bergmann, Rudolf Carnap, Philipp Frank, Carl Hempel, Hans Reichenbach, and Edgar Zilsel. Logical empiricism played a large role in shaping the contours of American academic philosophy, especially after World War II. Logical empiricism was central to the development of formal logic, metalogic, semantics and philosophy of language, philosophy of science, and (especially formal) epistemology. It was also important in the development of noncognitivism in ethics. The rise and flourishing of analytic philosophy in the United States, Britain, and then throughout the world depended upon the prominence of logical empiricism. By the same token, since the 1970s, if not before, analytic philosophy has understood itself to have progressed away from the doctrines and techniques of philosophy associated with logical empiricism. Logical empiricism was once an important movement within analytic philosophy and is now no longer a movement in analytic philosophy (or elsewhere).

This one-paragraph summation of logical empiricism is about as uncontroversial as any set of claims about the recent history of philosophy can be. Any reputable book-length history of analytic philosophy contains at least one chapter on logical empiricism.[1] Logical empiricism is, within such histories, associated with new logical techniques for doing philosophy as well as with certain fundamental, but ultimately naïve and mistaken philosophical doctrines – the verificationist theory of meaning, the rejection of metaphysics, the linguistic doctrine of logical truth, the claim that mathematics and logic are purely formal or analytic, and perhaps a few others. The chapters on logical empiricism in these histories typically have a common structure, then: they show the original relation of logical empiricism to other foundational projects in analytic philosophy and why the doctrines associated with logical empiricism have an initial attraction and, perhaps, plausibility, but then provide the decisive arguments against those doctrines. Armed with such arguments against such doctrines, rather than against a whole tradition of philosophizing, analytic philosophy continues past logical empiricism, absorbing both its useful technical advances and the rejection of its central doctrines. The next chapters of the histories often go to the work of those

---

[1] This framing has persisted for more than half a century; compare Passmore (1957), Stroll (2001), and Soames (2018).

associated with the anti-logical–empiricist arguments, usually Willard van Orman Quine, occasionally the late Ludwig Wittgenstein or Oxford ordinary language philosophy.

This Element will outline a different view. The problem is not so much that the other stories are wrong. In a real sense, the stories have become self-certifying: in virtue of being repeated for more than half a century these stories give an account of logical empiricism and its legacy that the vast majority of trained analytic philosophers take for granted. The influence logical empiricism has had for a couple of generations is largely the influence assigned to it by these stories. Nonetheless, the stories have been reconsidered recently from a variety of angles – there is now an enormous literature reevaluating logical empiricism.[2] Within this literature, for example, it has been disputed that logical empiricism is a project that can properly be connected to a few central doctrines such that, should these doctrines be refuted, the project is dead; against this, it has been noted that several of the core logical empiricists never adopted some of the alleged core doctrines or came to reject those doctrines while still thinking of themselves as pursuing the same overall philosophical project. This Element will deploy some of the central themes of the literature reappraising logical empiricism to offer a new account of the significance of logical empiricism for twentieth-century philosophy. This Element will take seriously (while lacking space to detail) both the range of different projects embedded within logical empiricism and the wealth of materials the logical empiricists drew upon within those projects. But it will, as it must, delimit the scope of its interests and concentrate on a few key figures and issues.

What Is Logical Empiricism? A First Account

In order to undertake the project of this Element, we of course need to know the referent and the meaning of the term "logical empiricism." We also need to draw out explicitly the largely implicit default story of logical empiricism that those trained in analytic philosophy imbibe in order to motivate a reappraisal.

In the matter of reference, matters are relatively straightforward. The groups who aligned themselves with the project were the members of the Vienna Circle and the Berlin Group associated with Hans Reichenbach (Milkov and Peckhaus 2013). The Vienna Circle is among the most famous groups of early twentieth-century philosophers. Its members also did the historian of logical empiricism the favor of writing a manifesto in which they explained their philosophical views and presented their membership this is the *Wissenschaftliche Weltauffassung (Scientific World-Conception)* of 1929 and produced several

---

[2] Major works in this reappraisal include Friedman (1999), Reisch (2005), Stadler (2015), and Uebel (2015).

participant histories (Neurath et al. [1929] 2012).[3] We will get to the vision of philosophy offered in the manifesto shortly. Here we will discuss briefly the membership circa 1929.

What in 1929 announced itself as the Vienna Circle began meeting in 1922 when the physicist-turned-philosopher Moritz Schlick arrived in Vienna to become the fourth occupant in the chair for philosophy of the inductive sciences, a chair that had been founded for Ernst Mach in 1895. The 1929 manifesto was written in celebration of Schlick's decision to stay in Vienna and thus to continue as the central figure around whom the Circle was organized. The principal authors of the manifesto were the philosopher Rudolf Carnap, the sociologist and political economist Otto Neurath, and the mathematician Hans Hahn (Uebel 2012). In addition to these four figures, the manifesto lists ten members of the Circle: Gustav Bergmann, Herbert Feigl, Philipp Frank, Kurt Gödel, Viktor Kraft, Karl Menger, Marcel Natkin, Olga Hahn-Neurath, Theodor Radakovic, and Friedrich Waismann. The number of intellectuals in Vienna who were associated with the Circle was much larger than this; Friedrich Stadler's definitive history of the Circle lists about twenty more figures who were in some way and at some point affiliated with the Circle (Stadler 2015).

The authors of the manifesto claimed that their project was an international movement and thus listed a group of figures "close to the Vienna Circle." These included the Berliners Walter Dubislav, Kurt Grelling, and Hans Reichenbach. They also listed several more Viennese scholars: the architect Josef Frank (Philipp's brother), Heinrich Loewy, and Edgar Zilsel. Rounding out this group, they listed Hasso Härlen of Stuttgart, Eno Kaila of Finland, Frank P. Ramsey of Cambridge, and Kurt Reidemeister of Koenigsberg. The pamphlet also listed Albert Einstein, Bertrand Russell, and Ludwig Wittgenstein as the "leading representatives of the scientific world conception." This provides us with a wide enough range of persons and views, although we need to make one addition: in 1929, Reichenbach's student Carl Hempel was too young to be well known to the Viennese authors of the manifesto. He would in time become one of the central figures in American logical empiricism, however.[4]

In an important sense, logical empiricism just is the philosophy presented and exemplified by these figures – at least for some period of their careers. This is not ordinarily, however, how we think of philosophical projects or schools of thought. We usually present them as content – we present their methods, goals, and tenets. This is how the default story of logical empiricism is told. We can

---

[3] See, for example, Joergenson (1951), the introduction to Frank (1951), and the first four essays in Feigl (1981).

[4] Hempel's classic essays are reprinted in Hempel (1965); his place in logical empiricism is outlined in Friedman (2000b).

approach the telling of this story through a few of the key documents in the articulation of logical empiricism.

Before we begin, we must deal with an initial complication. The project that came to be called "logical empiricism" had many names, even if we restrict our attention to those who identified with or endorsed the project. Within the Anglophone context, the first name associated with the project was "logical positivism," which was the term chosen by the young American recruit Albert Blumberg and Feigl in their 1931 introductory essay (Blumberg and Feigl 1931). Only about a decade later was that term routinely discarded in favor of "logical empiricism," a slight variation of a term ("logistic empiricism") introduced for an Anglophone audience by Reichenbach in the mid-1930s (Reichenbach 1936). For some of the figures in the movement, some of the names were importantly more accurate than others; other figures were indifferent to the question of naming. For some (such as Neurath), certain words (such as "philosophy") were dangerously vague or ambiguous and to be avoided. The change of names is sometimes itself marshaled as an argument for a degenerating trajectory: a robust anti-metaphysical positivist project became an increasingly diluted project of empiricism. I will continue to use "logical empiricism" as my main term – this was the term most used by adherents as the project gained prominence in the American context. But in this historical sketch, we must begin with "logical positivism" – a term that retains a strong presence in the wider academic world, especially among scientists and among those critical of positivism.

As just noted, the term "logical positivism" was first used in print to discuss the philosophy of the Vienna Circle in 1931 in an essay Blumberg and Feigl wrote for the *Journal of Philosophy*. Blumberg and Feigl introduce the term "logical positivism" with the following words: "To facilitate criticism and to forestall even more unfortunate attempts at labeling this aspect of contemporary European philosophy, we shall employ the term 'logical positivism.' Although it is perhaps the best among many poor ones, the name may suggest a mere rephrasing of traditional positivism. However, this is not the case" (Blumberg and Feigl 1931, pp. 281–282).

The term was meant to do two things: summarize the main features of the philosophy on offer, and suggest the relations of that philosophy to other historically given philosophical projects, especially positivism. Moreover, Blumberg and Feigl are clear that the term, while better than others they could think of, was not really adequate for the purposes for which it was introduced. Each of these aspects of the term deserves at least a bit more elaboration.

The first point speaks to the innovations of logical positivism as Blumberg and Feigl present it. One of the most interesting phenomena in recent European philosophy was, they argued, the convergence of two significant traditions: the positivistic-empirical and the logical. Comparable in importance to the Kantian synthesis of rationalism and empiricism, this new movement was sharply distinguished from Kantianism both by its results and by the fact that it embodies not the work of an individual, but the agreement of numerous logicians, philosophers, and scientists who independently arrived at the position.

Given this interpretative framework, the authors go on to argue that the epistemology of empirical knowledge, especially empirical science, has been the purview of empiricist epistemology, but this project has traditionally underestimated and misunderstood the nature and importance of logical and mathematical knowledge. Rationalism has been better at explaining mathematical and logical knowledge but has traditionally underestimated and misunderstood the nature and importance of empirical knowledge. Their logical positivism was the attempt, inspired by revolutionary new advances in the formal sciences and in the understanding of the methodology of exact physical science, to recombine in a non-Kantian way the insights of rationalism and empiricism and to understand the role of the formal sciences in empirical knowledge. Thus, the account at once paid homage to the significance of Kant's philosophical ambitions and acknowledged the failure of Kant's project adequately to fulfill those ambitions.

The choice of the term "logical positivism" expressed both the synthetic element of the project and a philosophical and historical connection to the project of nineteenth-century positivism. The "traditional" Machian positivism toward which the passage just quoted gestures was, crudely, an attempt to provide a generally empiricist experiential foundation to empirical scientific knowledge and to reject, as beyond our experiential ken, the claims of metaphysics. Thus, a Machian positivist would attempt to explain the nature of, say, knowledge of the physical world through attention to how physical concepts (such as force or mass or energy) organize the content of experience while claiming that notions such as cause or essence or ideal value go beyond what we can experience and thus should be rejected. Logic, within the project Blumberg and Feigl offer, will provide the purely formal framework within which to express the relations of scientific claims to experience. Moreover, the techniques of definition within modern formal logic provide, finally, a precise and general instrument to make exact the negative claim about metaphysics. By showing that the alleged claims of metaphysics contain concepts that cannot be defined on the basis of experience, logic can show exactly why such claims should be rejected: they are not rejected because they are false or subjective or dangerous but because they are, strictly speaking, meaningless.

Logic thus at once allows logical positivism to connect their technical concerns to traditional rationalism (while rejecting the synthetic a priori), fulfill the project of empiricist epistemology, clarify and discharge the anti-metaphysical tasks of positivism, and occupy a position within philosophy reminiscent of that claimed by Kant. It also does more than that. For, as the authors then detail, logic and mathematics both set and solve an epistemological problem within modern physical methodology that none of the previous projects could even express (Blumberg and Feigl 1931, pp. 288ff). A simplified version of the issue can be presented within the context of the question of whether physical space is Euclidean or non-Euclidean, a topic of significant import to logical positivism due to its centrality in the history of relativistic physics.[5]

Euclidean geometry differs from its non-Euclidean alternatives in many ways; importantly for our question, these geometries differ in their theorems about properties such as the angle-sum property for triangles and the ratio between the radius of a circle and its circumference. So, for example, in Euclidean (flat) geometry, all triangles have angles that sum to a straight angle or 180 degrees. In non-Euclidean geometries of constant negative curvature, all triangles have angles that sum to less than 180 degrees, and the difference between the sum and 180 degrees increases with the size of the triangle. Non-Euclidean geometries of constant positive curvature have angles that sum to more than 180 degrees, and the difference between the sum and 180 degrees increases with the size of the triangle. This suggests an empirical test regarding the geometry of physical space: given a big enough triangle, we should be able to discern whether the angles sum to 180 degrees or less or more than that. The great German mathematician Christian Gauss undertook such measurements using light beamed from mountaintops and discerned no divergence from Euclidean structure.

Logical positivism asks for philosophical care to be taken at just this point. Measuring the angles between light beams helps us determine the angle-sum property for physical triangles only if light travels in straight lines. How can you determine this? You could see if light can be beamed along the edge of a straightedge. But this again presumes that the straightedge is straight, and how do you determine that? Eventually, say the logical positivists, building on their understanding of the work of Einstein and Henri Poincaré ([1902] 2017), you get to a point where you cannot empirically check for physical straightness but rather must make a conventional choice about what you are going to count as straight. Within the parlance employed by Blumberg and Feigl, which they took from the work of Reichenbach, the scientist must make a conventional choice of

---

[5] The methodology of physics and the structure of physical space as understood by the logical empiricists in Einstein's wake is a huge topic. Key texts include Schlick ([1919] 1963), Reichenbach ([1920] 1965, [1928] 1958), and Carnap ([1922] 2019). See also Friedman (1983, chapter 1) and Ryckman (2005).

an axiom or definition of coordination (Blumberg and Feigl 1931, p. 289). What is coordinated is, on the one hand, an already well-defined mathematical concept or structure (straightest possible line, in the example) and, on the other, experientially available processes in the physical world (for example, the path of a light ray or a straightedge). Gauss, for example, instead of presuming that light travels in straight lines, should have said something like "I hereby choose 'path of a light ray' to be what 'physically straight line' means." Once you have done that you have a way to coordinate the experimental result with the theorems of the various geometries, and only then can you take yourself to be testing those geometries against facts given in experience at all.

In the example, the coordination is between a specific geometrical concept – a straight line – and a particular physical process – the path of light rays. The coordination could, however, be more global; one could decide, for example, that Euclidean geometry is the simplest to work with and, thus, that you wish to use it. You have thereby conventionally chosen a Euclidean structure for space. Any complications arising from this decision could be pushed into more and more complicated physics. There might be limits on how far you would want to go in this direction – Einstein himself objected to gravity conceived of as a universal force, preferring to alter the underlying space-time geometry. Similarly, certain circumstances might require violations of causal connection if a Euclidean space(-time) is chosen. But here too there are methodological trade-offs only, not demands offered to the very nature of experience, reason, or science. There is never a simple empirical refutation of an assertion about the metrical geometry of space(-time).

It is the novelty of this sort of epistemological problem – one not known to classical empiricism or nineteenth-century positivism – that explains the unhappiness Blumberg and Feigl have with their own chosen moniker, "logical positivism." Logical positivism was a philosophy of scientific knowledge as developed in close contact with revolutionary developments in the exact sciences and the issues raised were not the same as the epistemological problems central to the projects of traditional philosophy of any stripe. Rather, the most precise accounts of the epistemological problem and its solution were to be found in the methodological and scientific work of the exact scientists themselves, especially in the work of Einstein and Poincaré. The name "logical positivism" was a decidedly backward-looking name – a name that placed logical positivism in an historical development of philosophy – but the philosophy espoused was presented as revolutionary, as importantly unprecedented, as dependent on clarifications of the foundations of knowledge revealed in the then-contemporary revolutions in exact science.

The example of conventionalism in geometry gives a flavor of the revolutionary aspect of the scientific context within which the logical empiricists were working, but it surely does not provide anything approaching a synoptic vision.

Even in physics, there were other important elements to their interests in the content and methodology of new theories – questions of causation and determinism in quantum mechanics, the methods of metrology and operationalism, the questions of what counts, after the general theory of relativity, as giving a properly unified account of physical forces, and much more. Moreover, they were also interested in the revolutionary changes in mathematical logic and the conceptions of rigorous foundations of analysis as well as in arguably revolutionary changes in social science and psychology in the work of Max Weber, the behaviorists, and the Gestalt psychologists. Revolution in science and, for some of them, such as Neurath, also in politics, was very much in the air.

This revolutionary vision of logical empiricism is to be found not only in this introductory work by Blumberg and Feigl – such rhetoric abounds in the literature of logical empiricism of the time. It is evident in the aforementioned 1929 public announcement of the Vienna Circle, *Wissenschaftliche Weltauffassung*. In this work, the authors claimed that its philosophical work was revolutionary not merely in the details of the epistemological problem that it takes up, but also in its entire mode of philosophical inquiry, a mode that brings philosophy finally into the modern world and ties it to other socially progressive intellectual and practical movements. The revolutionary new philosophy espoused takes its place within science, not beyond it, and it serves not to limit the possibilities of scientific knowledge, but to foster them:

> *There is no such thing as philosophy as a basic or universal science alongside or above the various fields of the one empirical science*; there is no path to genuine knowledge other than the path of experience; there is no realm of ideas that stands over or beyond experience. Nevertheless, the work of "philosophical" or "foundational" investigations in the spirit of the scientific world-conception remains important. For the logical clarification of scientific concepts, propositions, and methods liberates one from inhibiting prejudices. Logical and epistemological analysis by no means wants to set limit scientific inquiry; on the contrary, analysis provides science with as complete a range of formal possibilities as is possible, from which to select what best fits each empirical finding (example: non-Euclidean geometries and the theory of relativity). (Neurath et al. [1929] 2012, p. 89; emphasis in the original)

Even Schlick, a more personally and politically conservative person than most of the logical empiricists, could not at this time contain his revolutionary rhetoric. He was given the first word in the logical empiricist house journal, *Erkenntnis*, in 1930 and chose for the title of his piece "Die Wende der Philosophie" ("The Turning Point in Philosophy"; Schlick ([1930] 1959). He placed his remarks within the context of a general concern about the objectivity and progress of philosophy, noting that many commentators on the history of philosophy have found it little more than a conflict of systems offered by individual philosophers and elaborated by schools devoted to those philosophers. In the essay, he cites a methodological advance as the reason philosophy circa 1930 is able to turn away from such a fruitless conflict of systems:

> I am convinced that we now find ourselves at an altogether decisive turning point in philosophy, and that we are objectively justified in considering that an end has come to the fruitless conflict of systems. We are already at the present time, in my opinion, in possession of methods which make every such conflict in principle unnecessary. What is now required is their resolute application. (Schlick [1930] 1959, p. 54)

This advance had two parts: the technical advances of formal logic and the epistemological advance in the understanding of the nature of logical truth. Regarding the latter, Schlick argued that once we understand logical (and mathematical) truth as purely formal, we can see that it is not a branch of science with its own special subject matter but rather a purely formal discipline that presents frameworks within which any knowledge of any subject can and must be couched. The philosophy of logical empiricism is simply the precise elaboration of logical systems for science.

Based on this exposition, we are now in a position to understand some of the core doctrines of logical empiricism, if not in their full technical detail, then in their philosophical motivations. Consider, for example, their commitment to there being a difference in principle between the nature of logico-mathematical truth and empirical truth. This commitment is embedded in the conventionalist story. That story begins with the various systems of metrical geometry having been fully developed as mathematical systems. For example, what a Euclidean straight line or a geodesic in a geometry of constant negative curvature is, is wholly a matter of mathematical definition. The ability of consistent axiom systems in mathematics to pick out structures that fulfill them is not in question; it is taken for granted. The question asked is how these mathematical structures are brought to bear on the world of matters of fact of experience in order to render possible a precise, predictive, mathematized knowledge of nature. But it is not just the truths of logic and mathematics that have this status of not having either truth makers in or confirmed by experience. Also, the conventions that connect the mathematics to the world of experience also have this epistemological status; the conventions are, in the very nature of the case, not empirically grounded but chosen. They can turn out to be simple or difficult to work with, but they cannot be confirmed or falsified. It is a further elaboration of this idea that led to the distinction between analytic and synthetic sentences within logically formalized languages, which is how the distinction between logico-mathematical truth, on the one hand, and empirical truth, on the other, ultimately is analyzed in logical empiricism beginning around 1930. The analytic/synthetic distinction is a way to make logically precise the informal epistemology on which the conventionalist methodology relies.[6]

Among the reasons to wish to convert the informal epistemology of conventionalism into a rigorous distinction of logical and methodological claims within science was a general distrust the logical empiricists had about philosophical vocabulary. This attitude is most prominently displayed in their efforts to show that metaphysical claims are meaningless. How might one in a rigorous fashion show that an allegedly meaningful concept (say, cause or essence) is meaningless? One idea would be this: begin with a language adequate for the description of experience, use the techniques of formal logic (already, as we have seen, shown to be analytic, meaningful but making no claims about the world of experience) to show how all other empirical concepts can be defined from the primitive terms of that description. This is one way to express the verificationist theory of empirical or cognitive meaningfulness: all empirical concepts are definable in a language of pure experience so that any empirical claim can be translated into a logically complicated statement in that language.[7] All statements of metaphysics can then be shown to be empirically meaningless by showing that they contain concepts undefinable in the language of experience. The claims of metaphysics defy any effort to regiment into a system of axioms connected by definition to experience. Nor, of course, do the metaphysicians think that they are doing merely formal work with concepts – they insist that they are making substantive statements about the world; metaphysics is not a branch of mathematics. The logical empiricists respond to this situation as follows: we respect the intention that metaphysics be a substantive discipline but as far as we can tell, given the failure to find a consistent set of definitions that tie such concepts to experience, metaphysicians do not succeed in actually making statements about the world. We eliminate metaphysics in this way; in order to avoid eliminating epistemology or philosophy of science along with metaphysics, it must be shown how to regiment the heretofore informal concepts of epistemology or methodology of science into logically precise concepts. What is not unclear about the a priori or the conventional is captured in the formal definition of analyticity for a language of science. This is Carnap's project in the logic of science.[8]

---

[6] We will return to this distinction and its critics in the section "Logical Empiricist Scientific Philosophy," where references to relevant literature are also provided.

[7] Perhaps no single issue in logical empiricism has generated as much literature as verificationism. Recent contextual discussions include Uebel (2015) and Verhaegh (2020).

[8] Carnap's first rigorous attempt at a logic of science is Carnap ([1934] 1937); he provided a more elementary account in Carnap (1935).

The Received Significance of Logical Empiricism

No story worth telling is a story simply of a project that was born, developed, and was superseded. If logical empiricism is worth caring about, there must be some account of the significance of it. The most salient stories of the significance of logical empiricism have framed that significance as a part of the development of the project of empiricism, on the one hand, or analytic philosophy, on the other. Often the two frames are combined.

This framing of the significance of logical empiricism is due largely to the logical empiricists themselves. We have already seen that Blumberg and Feigl presented logical empiricism (their "logical positivism") as a project that combined empiricism with a commitment to a formalist account of logical and mathematical truth. Even earlier, the Vienna Circle explained their philosophical work in similar ways. Already in 1929, in the *Wissenschaftliche Weltauffassung*, Neurath, Carnap, and Hahn explained their philosophical point of view this way:

> We have characterized the *scientific world-conception* essentially by *two features. First* it is *empiricist and positivist:* there is knowledge only from experience, which rests on what is immediately given. This sets the limits for the content of legitimate science. *Second*, the scientific world-conception is marked by the application of a certain method, namely that of *logical analysis*. The aim of scientific work is to reach the goal, unified science, by applying logical analysis to the empirical material. (Neurath et al. [1929] 2012, p. 84)

The most diligent framer of the history of logical empiricism within the history of empiricism is, however, perhaps logical empiricism's most famous critic, Quine. Much of Quine's work has a distinctively historical cast to it and throughout that work he is at pains to locate logical empiricism – especially Carnap's logical empiricism – within the larger project of empiricism tout court. Thus, for example, Quine's "Five Milestones of Empiricism" presents an entirely internal history of empiricism, starting from Locke and ending with Quine himself (Quine 1981). Along the way, the philosophy of the Vienna Circle is presented within the second milestone of empiricism, the move from concern with the meanings of words to the meanings of sentences. Even more crucial than the positive place for logical empiricism in Quine's story is the negative place for it. Each of the last three of Quine's milestones of empiricism are aspects of his own repudiation of Carnap: holism (the move of semantic concern from sentences to systems of sentences), monism (the repudiation of the analytic/synthetic distinction), and naturalism.

The significance of Carnap's philosophy is, throughout Quine's work, understood as a particular kind of effort to employ logic in the service of stringently empiricist epistemological goals. This is perhaps most evident in Quine's account of "Viennese philosophy" in the opening paragraphs of his essay "Carnap and Logical Truth" (Quine 1963). There Quine claims that one embarrassment for historical empiricism was mathematics, which seemed to have both a certainty and a distance from experience that traditional empiricism could not countenance. This empiricist puzzle about mathematics was precisely the problem the Vienna Circle proposed to solve through a new account of the nature of logical and mathematical truth. Quine explains as follows:

> What now of the empiricist who would grant certainty to logic, and to the whole of the mathematics, and yet would make a clean sweep of other non-empirical theories under the name of metaphysics? The Viennese solution to this nice problem was predicated on language. Metaphysics was meaningless through misuse of language; logic was certain through tautologous use of language. (Quine 1963, p. 386)

Quine calls the idea that logical truths are true in virtue of the meanings of terms "the linguistic doctrine of logical truth." Throughout the essay, he represents the doctrine as an "epistemological doctrine" – a doctrine in an empiricist epistemology of logic.

This understanding of logical empiricism is the framework also for Quine's most famous essay, "Two Dogmas of Empiricism," in which the analytic/synthetic distinction is presented as one of the dogmas of foundationalist empiricism (Quine 1951). Moreover, Quinean holism and its consequences, monism and naturalism, are also, in Quine's account, in the service of empiricism. Quine's is of course a de-dogmatized empiricism. No longer does the empiricist philosopher feel embarrassed by mathematics, which is now recognized not as a priori at all, but merely as at quite a large remove from experience. There is no longer in Quinean empiricism a distinctive class of analytic sentences that achieve their truth in a uniquely nonempirical way. Indeed, as Quine presents it, monism follows from empiricism directly once a moderate holism regarding theory testing is accepted. Empiricism assigns to sentences only their empirical consequences as their meanings, but holism reminds us that no sentence by itself has any significant empirical consequences. Thus, there is nothing to assign as the meaning of an individual sentence. The empirical significance of a large enough chunk of theory can still be given; what cannot be done is to divvy up that significance sentence by sentence in order to arrive at the empirical meaning of each individual claim. Thus, since analytic sentences were supposed to differ from synthetic sentences in having no empirical meaning, our conclusion (no assignable empirical meaning for any sentence) gives us no way to delimit the class of analytic sentences.

While the largest feature of Quine's account of logical empiricism is its place within the history of empiricism, another historical narrative is also in play in Quine's work. Quine presents an empiricist epistemology at the heart of analytic philosophy. Thus, on Quine's view, Carnap's empiricist epistemological project in his 1928 *Der logische Aufbau der Welt* (Carnap [1928] 1961a) derives from the empiricist epistemology of Bertrand Russell's External World Program: "To account for the external world as a logical construct of sense data – such, in Russell's terms was the program. It was Carnap, in his *Der logische Aufbau der Welt* of 1928, who came closest to executing it" (Quine 1969, p. 74). More generally, Quine assimilates, in his "Five Milestones," the logical and semantical doctrines of Frege, Russell, and Wittgenstein, to the epistemological project of empiricism. Thus, Quine invites us to read logical empiricism as an episode also in the history of analytic philosophy. It is just that Quine's analytic philosophy is continuous with an empiricist epistemological tradition that went right back into the seventeenth century.

Rethinking the Significance of Logical Empiricism

So far, with very few exceptions, I have used the phrase "logical empiricism" in the singular, and surely logical empiricism has some form of unity. But the recent interpretative literature has argued that one way in which the standard story is impoverished is that takes logical empiricism to be a vastly more monolithic project than it actually was. The standard history, implicitly or explicitly, makes Carnap the central figure in logical empiricism. Carnap is clearly the main target of Quine's criticisms. Sometimes Quine seems to invite his readers to equate logical empiricism with Carnap's philosophy. When, for example, the failure of the analytic/synthetic distinction to do some epistemological work is taken as a refutation of all of logical empiricism, crucial differences between Carnap's and the other logical empiricist projects are often elided. Partially in response to this problem of interpretation and partially simply to recover interesting philosophical voices, there has arisen a literature that seeks to emphasize other versions of logical empiricism, often arguing that those versions do not suffer from the same philosophical problems that the Carnapian version does.

Within this literature of recovery, Neurath's logical empiricism is often given pride of place.[9] Quine offered naturalism as the replacement project within empiricism for Carnapian formalism; Neurath is of immediate interest for Quine's story, then, because he offered a naturalistic version of logical

---

[9] See, among others, Nemeth (1981), Haller (1993), Cartwight et al. (1996), Reisch (2005), Uebel (2015), Cat and Tuboly (2019).

empiricism right back into the 1920s. Moreover, Quine knew this and chose one version of Neurath's famous boat metaphor as the motto of his *Word and Object* (Quine 1960). This raises interesting questions about how one can be both a naturalist and a logical empiricist – Neurath seems not ever to have endorsed the two dogmas of empiricism that are the key to overcoming logical empiricism. The reintroduction into historical consciousness of Neurath's project cannot help but complicate the standard history of logical empiricism.

Neurath is interesting in other, not unrelated, ways also in complicating the standard history of logical empiricism. Neurath was a social scientist and both his sense of science and his main areas of interest in philosophy of science stemmed from his training in political economy and sociology. He also was a scholar of history, including history of science. He wrote papers in history of economics and history of physics. Neurath was also a deeply politically engaged and explicitly Austro-Marxist thinker and actor. Neurath clashed with both Carnap and Schlick on the evidentiary role of experience and the foundations of empirical knowledge in the protocol sentence debate. Thus, the aims and the methods of Neurath's logical empiricism do not seem the same as those we have come to associate with default logical empiricism. This difference between Neurath's and more technical logical empiricisms is thematized already in the 1929 manifesto:

> The scientific world-conception is close to the life of the present. Certainly it will face hard battles and hostility . . . Of course not every single adherent of the scientific world-conception will be a fighter. Some, glad of solitude, will lead a withdrawn existence on the icy slopes of logic; some may even disdain mingling with the masses and regret the "trivialization" which is inevitable when popularizing. (Neurath et al. [1929] 2012, p. 90)

It would seem, therefore, if logical empiricism is to accommodate both Carnap and Neurath, it will have to be a fairly broad-church movement, not one easily codified into a few shared philosophical doctrines and methods. Again, not only does Neurath complicate the picture for the historian, he thematizes this complication in his own work. Neurath decried any attempt to reduce logical empiricism to a list of agreed-upon philosophical theses: "A program formed of statements accepted by all collaborators would be narrow and would be a source of divergences in the near future . . . The maximum of co-operation – that is the program!" (Neurath 1938, pp. 23–24). His complicated understanding of the unity of the sciences was also exemplified – not accidentally – in his understanding of the complexities of the unity of logical empiricism itself.[10]

---

[10] See the several essays dedicated to unified science and encyclopedism collected in Neurath (1983).

Of course, adding Neurath's voice to the history of logical empiricism is merely a first step toward diversifying our understanding of the project. As noted earlier, Stadler (2015) lists more than thirty members of the Vienna Circle with many more allied persons in Vienna and abroad. The Vienna Circle by the early 1930s had room within it for, for example, explicitly Wittgensteinian philosophers such as Schlick and his assistant Friedrich Waismann, philosophers influenced by phenomenology such as Felix Kaufmann, and the Marxist historian of science and intellectual historian Edgar Zilsel, as well as figures, including the logician Kurt Gödel, the mathematicians Hans Hahn and Karl Menger, and the physicist Philipp Frank, whose largest contributions, at least early in their careers, were mainly in scientific disciplines. The Vienna Circle had considerable contact with other philosophical and scientific figures such as Karl Popper, the psychologists Karl Bühler and Egon Brunswik, the historian of philosophy Heinrich Gomperz, and the architect Josef Frank. In Berlin, Hempel eventually received his doctoral degree, after Reichenbach's forced removal with the rise of Nazism, under the direction of the eminent Gestalt psychologist Wolfgang Köhler. Reichenbach himself was hired into the physics faculty at Berlin in 1926 and had considerable contact with psychologists in Berlin, especially Kurt Lewin. Finding a common core of philosophical theses definitive of logical empiricism, given this diversity, seems unlikely, probably simply wrongheaded.

Attention to the variety of projects that the logical empiricists undertook or allied themselves with has been instrumental in loosening the hold of the standard story, at least among scholars of the movement. From this perspective, the standard story is not so much a general report on the influence of logical empiricism on philosophy as a lesson drawn by analytic philosophers about logical empiricism's importance for the development of analytic philosophy. This being the case, the standard story is less explanatory than in need of explanation: How and why did logical empiricism come to be reduced from the various and disparate elements it had in the European context to a narrow and specifically formalistic project that can be neatly slotted into a history of analytic philosophy? Did the diverse figures within logical empiricism come to understand the significance of their philosophies in terms of the advancement of logical analysis and empiricism, when, and why? Why did the socially active aspect of logical empiricism announced in 1929 fall away? From the broader viewpoint of historically available options for logical empiricism, the standard story now appears as deeply contingent, even surprising, not the inevitable working out of the problems with a few original and core logical empiricist doctrines.

Another, more directly conceptual historicist issue intersects with the literatures of complication and also suggests that the standard story of logical empiricism ought to have the status of a problem rather than a solution. As we have seen, the standard story trades in two principal philosophical notions, empiricism and analytic philosophy. Any reasonable historicism asks us, when presented with an account of a project, X, by placing it in a tradition, Y, to ask whether and to what extent Y can do that work. In the case of logical empiricism, the two frames suffer from different but ultimately similar important problems.

To illustrate this issue, let us limit our attention now mainly to Carnap and Reichenbach and ask after the interpretative issues with locating their work wholly within the context of empiricism. A number of scholars have argued in various ways that Carnap's early philosophical work showed the strong influence of scientific neo-Kantianism of the Marburg school. While Carnap did believe that the *Aufbau* importantly differed from the neo-Kantian epistemology on offer in Germany in the 1910s and 1920s, we should not be surprised to find some major themes of that epistemology central to Carnap's project. Among the debts to neo-Kantianism one can find in Carnap's early work is the centrality of logic in the epistemology of the empirical sciences. For example, Ernst Cassirer's understanding of the post-Kantian problem of knowledge indicated that what needed to be shown was how the intellectual constructions of logic and mathematics were precisely the basis upon which objective empirical knowledge of the world was built. It was in this way that Cassirer both secured the exact sciences of nature as the proper topic of epistemology and reoriented the business of epistemology to showing how the form of experience allowed the mathematically precise statement of natural laws.[11]

In Carnap's earliest work, starting from his dissertation, *Der Raum* (Carnap [1922] 2019), other philosophical and nonempiricist influences are just as clear. In the dissertation, Carnap speaks in Kantian language, calling our knowledge of the structure of intuitive space synthetic a priori knowledge. But his official account of the foundations of our knowledge of intuitive space is explicitly indebted to phenomenology; he explains our knowledge of intuitive space using Edmund Husserl's notion of *Wesensschau*. In the *Aufbau*, there is no longer any need for *Wesensschau*, but arguably the naming of the overarching philosophical framework of the work "constitution theory" is a nod to the constitution theory of Husserl's *Ideen*. We know that Carnap joined Husserl's advanced seminar in phenomenology briefly between writing his dissertation and publishing the *Aufbau*; we know that the largest project within the Husserl circle at the time was the preparation of the second volume of *Ideen*; it would be surprising if nothing from that context played an important role in Carnap's understanding of what he was doing.[12]

---

[11] Cassirer (1910); on Cassirer on scientific knowledge, see Richardson (1998, chapter 3), Friedman (1999, chapters 5 and 6, 2000a), the papers in part 1 of Friedman and Luft (2015), and Matherne (2021, chapters 3 and 4).

[12] On Husserl and Carnap, see, among others, Sarkar (2003), Ryckman (2008), and Carus (2016).

The language that both Carnap and Reichenbach used to describe the lessons of the relativity theory in the early 1920s was Kantian. For Reichenbach (1920), the lesson to be learned was that Kant had conflated two notions of the synthetic a priori – "constitutive of the object of knowledge" and "necessary and universal." Relativity theory had principles constitutive of the object of knowledge and, in this sense, the synthetic a priori had not only survived the shift to contemporary physics, but had also been clarified by that shift. What could no longer be endorsed was any sense of the synthetic a priori that made it universal, necessary, and unchanging. This "relativized a priori" is also on offer in Carnap's dissertation, in his account of the structure of physical space. It had also been expressed in the epistemology of the exact sciences Cassirer provided in 1910 in his *Substanzbegriff und Funktionsbegriff*.[13]

If we cast our intellectual nets even wider, we find a number of other philosophical and cultural influences on Carnap and Reichenbach's early work that might well have left a lingering mark. Reichenbach, during his student days, was a socialist, a pacifist, and an activist within the *Freistudenten* movement in Berlin. Carnap also had a political background that included membership as a youth in the utopian nature society, the *Wandervögel*, and a lingering political-cum-philosophical commitment to a form of expressivism about philosophy influenced by his professors and ultimately by Wilhelm Dilthey's *Weltanschauungslehre*. The political and cultural projects of the logical empiricists lingered into the era of the Vienna Circle. Neurath, Carnap, and Frank all lectured at the Dessau Bauhaus and claimed a kinship between logical empiricist philosophy and modern movements in art and architecture. Many of the logical empiricists also engaged in adult education at the *Wiener Volkshochschule*.[14]

What is the significance of these considerations? It is at least this: "empiricism" was a contested actors' category for the logical empiricists. It can be deployed to understand their work only if we take for granted changes they themselves wrought in the notion of empiricism or if we speak at such a high level of abstraction that the detailed texture of the history of empiricism is no longer discernible. For Carnap and Reichenbach, the voyage to empiricism was a complicated one. It was not at all clear through the mid-1920s for the logical empiricists themselves that a plausible story existed that tied the methodological lessons of Poincaré and Einstein to any extant form of empiricism. As outlined previously, in the language of Reichenbach's *Philosophie der Raum-Zeit-Lehre* (Reichenbach [1928] 1958), axioms of coordination are constitutive of the meanings of physical notions like "straightest line in space-time" in virtue

---

[13] On the relativized a priori, see Friedman (1999, chapter 3), Howard (2010), and Padovani (2011).

[14] On the larger social context for logical empiricism with particular reference to Carnap, see Galison (1996), Carus (2007), and Damböck et al. (2021).

of relating such notions to already well-defined mathematical structures. Those structures are themselves well behaved on logical grounds independently of experience, suggesting a robust notion of the mathematical a priori, and relating such structures to the facts of experience is what first makes objective physical science possible, which points to a lingering commitment to the methodological point – if not the vocabulary – of Kant's synthetic a priori.

Nonetheless, by the time Reichenbach wrote that book, he and, more problematically, Carnap did think of themselves as empiricists. This is not a triumph of the standard story of logical empiricism, however, since that story gives us no purchase on how that could have happened. No empiricist epistemology available before logical empiricism can absorb the lessons of conventionalism very readily; nor was their work always motivated by an effort to find a version of empiricism that could absorb those lessons. That much was obvious to Carnap and Reichenbach in the early 1920s. In 1923, for example, while he was already at work on the *Aufbau*, the work Quine takes to the high-water mark of traditional empiricist epistemology, Carnap wrote an essay in which he declared that empiricism was a nonstarter as an epistemology of the exact sciences. This essay, entitled "On the Task of Physics and the Application of the Axiom of Simplicity," begins:

> After a long period during which the question of sources of physical knowledge has been hotly disputed, it may now perhaps be said that pure empiricism has lost its dominance. That the construction of physics cannot rely solely on the results of experiments, but must use non-experiential principles, has of course been proclaimed by philosophy for some time now. But solutions that could satisfy the physicist resulted only after representatives of the exact sciences began to investigate the character of physical method, and arrived at a non-empiricist conception about it. (Carnap [1923] 2019a, p. 211)

In that essay, the principle of simplicity is the non-experiential principle under discussion. That principle serves as a formal constraint on theory choice in Carnap's account of physical methodology. The principle guides our sense of what is a proper scientific theory but is not itself grounded in experiment or experience. True to his own sense of the history of nonempiricist philosophy, Carnap's main business in the essay is to try to come up with a mathematically precise version of the axiom of simplicity, one that could satisfy the mathematicians and the physicists. Reichenbach dealt with similar issues in his dissertation in 1916, which addressed a specifically Kantian concern: the necessity of mathematics in the objective representation of nature (Reichenbach [1916] 2008).

In order subsequently to think of himself as an empiricist, Carnap had to convince himself that he was wrong about the lessons of exact science in the early twentieth century, that he had a faulty understanding of empiricism, or that a rigorously defensible notion of empiricism had not yet been but could be formulated. He chose the last of these options. But this is as much as to say that for him, as for Reichenbach, the notion of empiricism is itself in flux and contested throughout the 1920s – and, in Carnap's case at least, well into the 1930s. Thus "empiricist epistemology" is not a transparent explanatory frame within which to place their philosophical work. Empiricism itself had to change importantly in order for logical empiricism ultimately to be seen even by some of its practitioners as an empiricist philosophy. Any account of the significance of logical empiricism needs to take empiricism as itself an historical topic, not as an always already present philosophical framework.

The problems are similar for analytic philosophy as a frame for the account. Not least among the problems is the idea that analytic philosophy was a particularly friendly philosophical project for empiricism. None of the leading founders of analytic philosophy as we understand it today – Gottlob Frege, Bertrand Russell, and Ludwig Wittgenstein – is obviously an empiricist in a classical sense. Frege, who was a professor of Carnap, was clearly opposed to a Kantian understanding of arithmetic but his logicist program did not support an empiricist account of arithmetic. He was withering in his criticisms of the empiricist account of arithmetic of J. S. Mill (Frege [1884] 1960). Moreover, Frege retained the language of the synthetic a priori in speaking about geometry and, after Russell's criticisms of his version of the laws of logic, reintroduced such talk for arithmetic as well.

Russell's External World Program (Russell [1914] 1993), which sought, as Quine said, to account for the objects of physics as logical constructions of sense-data, sounds like an empiricist project. But, as Quine understood, whether and how it is an empiricist project depends upon the epistemological status of the logical tools Russell brings to bear in the project. On this matter, Russell is not clearly an empiricist. Very early, Russell, having disputed Kant's understanding of mathematics as synthetic a priori knowledge by showing how to reduce all of mathematics to logic, ended up saying that logical principles are themselves synthetic a priori. Later he deployed his basic epistemological notion of acquaintance and claim that we are acquainted not just with sense-data (and concepts) but also with logical primitives. This idea of a direct rational acquaintance with logical primitives is distinctly nonempiricist, philosophically obscure, and antithetical to the accounts of logic for which the logical empiricists became famous.

The Vienna Circle famously read Wittgenstein's *Tractatus Logico-Philosophicus* (Wittgenstein [1921] 1961) as a successor project to the Russell's External World Project. Again, however, the question is whether the account of logic given in the *Tractatus* can plausibly be thought to be friendly to empiricism. The *Tractatus* itself is silent on that issue; the term "empiricism" is not found in the text. For Carnap, the *Tractatus* provides a large step in the direction of his later views – views he came to think of as empiricist – by suggesting that logical truth was in principle different from empirical truth not in being absolutely general (pertaining to everything), but in being, so to speak, encoded into language. Logic on this view is both content-free and operational. The road here is open to a view in which, again as Quine says, logic is vouchsafed as a priori because it says nothing about the world and that this account is an answer to the question of an account of the a priority of mathematics that an empiricist can embrace. Two questions remain for this as the road Carnap takes. First, can the view of logic be made sense of on its own terms? (And, of course, that it cannot is precisely Quine's point in the analytic/synthetic debate.) Second, can logic so understood be made to do all the epistemic work that the logical empiricists see the formal doing to in methodology of empirical science? It is this second question and its complications that indicate to some that Carnap's views of logic retain much of the transcendental flavor of neo-Kantian views. Logic, philosophy of logic, logical analysis, understandings of the virtues of philosophy that limits itself to such tools – all these are also in flux in Carnap's work. Historically and hermeneutically, deploying an inchoate notion of "analytic philosophy" as a way to understand Carnap's work is explanatorily inert: he was attempting to find a notion of logic or analysis that could play the philosophical role he needed it to play.

The point can be put plainly: there was no canonical analytic tradition available for the early logical empiricists to endorse circa 1920 or 1930. Insofar as analytic philosophy became a philosophical tradition, it became one in part in and through the development of logical empiricism itself. Logical empiricism is undoubtedly important for the history of empiricism and the history of analytic philosophy. We cannot, however, explain the development of logical empiricism by seeing it as the ever more clear expression of a fundamental drive among the logical empiricists to be empiricists or to be analytic philosophers. That is a sort of teleological history that trades in unclear philosophical notions that the logical empiricists claimed to abjure and that, I will argue, misrepresents the most fundamental philosophical purpose of their work, and most emphatically the work of Carnap and Reichenbach.

The larger frame within which I place logical empiricism comes directly from its own motivating literature: logical empiricism was, in its development, a series of episodes and projects within the history of scientific philosophy. Throughout their early motivational literature, the logical empiricists were largely united and at pains to offer up logical empiricism as a way to make philosophy scientific or to offer a scientific successor to philosophy, to introduce the intellectual standards of the sciences into the morass of philosophy. Despite all their differences of detail in both topic and method of philosophy, this point was held substantially in common. Moreover, in the first years of logical empiricism's move to North America, it was received at least among some prominent American philosophers as a project in scientific philosophy. Within the North American context, it was only in the years after World War II that the story of logical empiricism was told more or less exclusively as an episode in an Anglo-American project of analytic philosophy.

The notion of a scientific philosophy that includes logical empiricism may sound odd to some philosophical ears. Some will think that whatever philosophy is or may be, it is not a science. Indeed, within the analytic context, it is mainly contemporary naturalists, who view themselves as far from logical empiricism, who think that philosophy either does or should take its place among the sciences. The broad disappearance of a scientific ambition for philosophy even within analytic philosophy, together with the sense that naturalistic scientific philosophy is a rejection of the central philosophical features of logical empiricism, are themselves aspects of the contemporary framework of analytic philosophy that cry out for historical explanation. For not a hundred years ago, many who came to be seen as founders of analytic philosophy and many other philosophers were united in seeking to make philosophy a scientifically responsible endeavor and offered several non-naturalistic alternatives.

In placing the history of logical empiricism within the framework of scientific philosophy, I am undertaking an historicist project, seeking to express the motivations and significance of the project in terms that its historical advocates took seriously. Historicism is also not good simply for its own sake. I believe, however, that this change in framework does real historical and philosophical work. In the next section, I further specify the larger project of scientific philosophy and develop aspects of the family of logical empiricist versions of it. In the final section, I use logical empiricism as scientific philosophy to reorient some philosophical and historical understandings of the development of twentieth-century philosophy.

Logical Empiricism As Scientific Philosophy: Evidence and Background

Any new account of the significance of logical empiricism needs to seek a more fundamental philosophical commitment within it than a commitment to empiricism or to analytic methods in philosophy or to specific doctrines associated with those commitments (verificationism, the linguistic doctrine of logical truth). It is for this reason that I introduced at the end of the previous section the notion of scientific philosophy. The interpretative idea is that the commitment to introduce scientific methods, goals, and processes within philosophy is the most fundamental joint commitment of the logical empiricists. We cannot expect too much of this interpretation – it would be ill conceived to attempt to reunify into a tidy intellectual package all the disparate elements that the new literature of the varieties of logical empiricism has brought to our scholarly attention. Nonetheless, there is no doubt that there was among the logical empiricists a sense of a unified movement, despite the differences of opinion they had on many – perhaps all – doctrinal matters. It is the business of this section to advance this interpretation and to argue that within the Austrian and German contexts where logical empiricism arose, scientific philosophy, not analytic philosophy, not positivism, not empiricism, is the most apposite framework for understanding the philosophical project of logical empiricism.

Before continuing, however, we must take a brief detour through a terminological issue that arises from the fact that the early work of the logical empiricists is written in German. The standard German word for science is *Wissenschaft*; this is the word the logical empiricists use to refer to science. *Wissenschaft* in German is a broader term than is the English word "science." Thus, for example, the program of any humanities conference in Germany might well be called *der wissenschaftliche Programm* – the scientific program; it would never be called this in English. In general, any systematic study or body of knowledge is routinely called a *Wissenschaft* in German. Thus, when we attend to the use of *Wissenschaft* and *wissenschaftlich* and other cognate terms in German, we have to bear in mind that the term is more catholic in application.

This reminder is important because I will argue that the word *Wissenschaft* as employed in the early literature of the logical empiricists is more in line with the English usage of "science" than with the standard German usage. This desire for a stricter application of the term is indicated in the fact that when they are being careful about their terms, the logical empiricists (and others in the German-language philosophical world of the time) modify the word with adjectives such as *streng* or *exakt* – "strict" or "exact." Such words indicate that what is at stake is the question of whether and how philosophy might be scientific in the sense of the most exact sciences, the paradigmatic formal and natural sciences, which for the logical empiricists were certainly mathematics and physics. The issue of whether philosophy can be a science, then, is not answered by pointing out that all the humanities disciplines are, after all, *Wissenschaften* in the standard usage of the German term. The question is whether philosophy can be a science in a way that makes it as strictly or exactly scientific as mathematics or physics.

Some Evidence

The hortatory writings of the logical empiricists from the late 1920s and the early 1930s make clear that the primary purpose of the movement was to radically revise the practice and goals of philosophy so that it could participate in modern intellectual life and promote positive social values. This is evident whenever the logical empiricists pause from doing philosophy to discuss what they are doing as philosophers. Their remarks on this topic were clear and frequent. Philosophy had not managed to organize itself as a science; philosophers had not taken on the intellectual responsibility adopted by the scientist. Philosophy was, for these reasons, mired in fruitless debates in which personal opinions were presented as factual claims but lacked rational persuasiveness. There were no common standards, no common understanding of the vocabulary of philosophy. There was no way forward in philosophy without a radical reform motivated by and emulating the practices of those scientists who had made the clearest progress, mathematicians and physicists.

The Vienna Circle's manifesto, *Wissenschaftliche Weltauffassung*, announced in its very title the point of view motivating the philosophical project on offer. The idea was to bring philosophy fully into an already existing, indeed widespread, scientific outlook upon the world. The manifesto argued that it was principally in philosophy and theology that an opposition to a scientific conception of the world was to be found. Thus, it was important not just for philosophy but for the fully rational functioning of society that a scientific philosophy be developed. More than this, the manifesto ascribed the rise of metaphysical theorizing in the postwar era precisely to the critical social and economic troubles of the times. At stake was the fully conscious acceptance of scientific modernity:

> The increase in metaphysical and theologizing leanings which shows itself today in many associations and sects, in books and journals, in lectures and university courses, seems to be based on the fierce social and economic struggles of the present. One group of combatants, holding fast to traditional social forms, cultivates traditional attitudes of metaphysics and theology whose content has long since been superseded; while the other group, especially in central Europe, facing the new age, rejects these views and adopts empirical science as its basis. (Neurath et al. ([1929] 2012, p. 90)

Neurath's socialist leanings are clearly in view in such passages – the paragraph in fact ends with the claim that the scientific world conception was the most adequate expression of the down-to-earth empiricism and materialism of "the masses." What is crucial is the conservative social role ascribed to metaphysical philosophy: metaphysics is inherently connected with outmoded social forms and institutions. This view was not simply strategic or based on a wish to find some connection between old philosophy and old social forms. As Fritz Ringer (1969) and others have pointed out, academic philosophy had been important in the nineteenth century in the cementing of the German social and political order. This social role for philosophy was, just at the time of the Vienna Circle's manifesto, being rethought and curtailed; part of the crisis of Germanophone philosophy after World War I was precisely over the role philosophy should play socially.

At the time in Germany and Austria, there was a robust alternative to scientific philosophy – *Lebensphilosophie* – philosophy of life or life philosophy. It is not easy to describe *Lebensphilosophie* in short compass but, as the name suggests, it was understood (at least by its advocates) as a form of philosophy devoted to living a good, proper, or authentic life. It was less concerned with philosophy as a body of doctrine or a method for acquiring knowledge than as a source of practical wisdom. This sort of philosophy was in most of its varieties understood to be a non- or even anti-rationalist movement. Max Scheler ([1913] 2018) credited three thinkers as giving rise to *Lebensphilosophie*: Wilhelm Dilthey, Friedrich Nietzsche, and Henri Bergson. Bergson's notion of intuitive metaphysics – a metaphysical insight into the being of a thing, as it were, from the inside – was clearly at issue in the manifesto even though Bergson's name went unmentioned: "The view which attributes to intuition a superior and more penetrating power of knowing, capable of leading beyond the contents of sense experience and not to be confined by the shackles of conceptual thought – this view is rejected" (Neurath et al. ([1929] 2012, pp. 83–84). Indeed the joint insistence upon sensation as the material of all cognition – and thus empiricism – and logic as the conditions of rational thought was very much in opposition to a metaphysics based on intuition advanced by Bergson and adopted by some *Lebensphilosophen*. Carnap, for example, in the final part of his 1928 *Logischer Aufbau* (Carnap [1928] 1961a, §182) rejects metaphysics as meaningless, having adopted, for the purposes of this argument, a Bergsonian understanding of metaphysics as thought inexpressible in symbols (Bergson [1903] 1999). The philosophical tropes and social concerns of *Lebensphilosophie* also give shape to the final paragraph of the Vienna Circle's *Aufruf*, indicating that the goals of *Lebensphilosophie* are fulfilled more by scientific philosophy:

> Thus, the scientific world conception is close to the life of the present . . . We are witnessing how the spirit of the scientific world conception penetrates in growing measure the forms of personal and public life, of education, of child-rearing, of architecture, and how it helps shape economic and social life according to rational principles. *The scientific world-conception serves life, and life embraces it.* (Neurath et al. [1929] 2012, p. 90)

It has become clear in recent scholarship that the connection drawn in the *Wissenschaftlicher Weltauffassung* between logical empiricism and other modernist movements in education, architecture, and so forth was not simply a matter of motivating rhetoric; it was a program of activity.[15] Several Vienna Circle members were teachers in experimental educational settings such as the Vienna *Hochschule*, a generally socialist adult education project. Josef Frank, the brother of Philipp, was a leading modernist architect in Vienna. Several members of the Vienna Circle, including Feigl, Neurath, and Carnap, gave lectures at the Dessau Bauhaus. Neurath was throughout his life fervently involved in educational projects that incorporated what we would now call "new information technologies" such as his ISOTYPE method for the visual representation of scientific information. The same is true in Berlin of Hans Reichenbach and his activities on radio. Neurath was also an urban planner, museum curator, and, briefly, a minister for economic rationalization in the Soviet Republic of Bavaria.[16] The Vienna Circle itself had a public outreach arm in the Ernst Mach Society, which sponsored public lectures on topics in science and scientific philosophy in Vienna. The manifesto makes plain that such activities are not add-ons but essential to the philosophy on offer:

> The Vienna Circle does not rest content with collective work as a closed group. It is also trying to make contact with the active movements of the present, insofar as they are well disposed toward the scientific world-conception and turn away from metaphysics and theology ... The Vienna Circle believes that in collaborating with the Ernst Mach Society it fulfills a demand of the day: we have to fashion intellectual tools for everyday life, for the daily life of the scholar but also for the daily life of all those who in some way join in working at the conscious reshaping of life. The vitality that shows itself in the efforts for a rational transformation of the social and economic order, permeates the movement for a scientific world-conception also. (Neurath et al. [1929] 2012, p. 81)

In other passages in which the logical empiricists sought to motivate their project, the focus is mainly on the internal reshaping of the discipline of philosophy. The logical empiricists had a diagnosis of the lack of intellectual authority from which philosophy suffered. It stemmed from an improper understanding of the nature of knowledge production. Philosophy had always, especially in metaphysical ages, been understood as the expression of a sort of personal genius or special wisdom of the individual philosopher. In this philosophy was more like poetry or other creative arts than like science – yet

---

[15] See especially the details of the activities of the Vienna Circle in Stadler (2015).

[16] On Neurath, see Cartwright et al. (1996) and Cat and Tuboly (2019); for Reichenbach, see Richardson (2021).

philosophy, unlike poetry or art, wished to present itself as a form of knowledge. What philosophy needed to do to fulfill its ambitions was to have a different model of the epistemic agent, a model taken from the proper operation of the scientific research community. This piecemeal collaborative aspect of the new scientific philosophy is the most important point that Carnap makes in the introduction to his *Aufbau*. When joined into a genuine research community, philosophers behave differently and can expect more lasting results:

> The individual no longer undertakes to erect in one bold stroke an entire system of philosophy. Rather, each works at his special place with the one unified science. For the physicist and the historian this orientation is commonplace, but in philosophy we witness the spectacle (which must be depressing to a person of scientific orientation) that one after another and side by side a multiplicity of incompatible philosophical systems is erected. If we allot to the individual in philosophical work as in the special sciences only a partial task, then we can look forward with more confidence into the future: in slow careful construction insight after insight will be won. (Carnap ([1928] 1961a, pp. xvi–xvii)

For Hans Reichenbach, in 1929, the very idea that philosophers engaged in something properly called "research" was new and bold, an indication that such philosophy had taken its stand within the special scientific disciplines. He too argued that this stance differed in principle from a social organization around a few great figures in the history of philosophy – or around a single philosophy professor in a German university. Such a philosophy of schools or movements – such as an early twentieth-century configuration of German philosophy into various sects of neo-Kantians or neo-Hegelians – was antithetical to proper epistemic functioning. Such an organization of philosophy was, for Reichenbach, a sort of "unproductive epigonism the sight of which must repel anyone who works in the stimulating atmosphere of the sciences and who has even once looked at contemporary philosophy from this vantage point" (Reichenbach [1929] 1978, p. 250).

This rhetoric is perhaps surprising, since the *Wissenschaftliche Weltauffassung* was written in celebration of Schlick's decision to remain in Vienna rather than take up the chair in philosophy at Bonn. Similarly, the decision to name the public wing of Vienna Circle activities after Mach might suggest a mere school of thought – a group of neo-Machians to add to the neo-Kantians, neo-Friesians, and all the rest. In the case of Mach and the Verein Ernst Mach, the manifesto is explicit: "By the choice of its name, the society wishes to describe its basic orientation: science free of metaphysics. This, however, does not mean that the society declares itself to be in programmatic agreement with the individual doctrines of Mach" (Neurath et al. [1929] 2012, p. 81). This message had been underscored already in the text by the enormous array of influences listed earlier in the first section of the work – in all the names of more than forty scientists and philosophers are mentioned, stretching from Epicurus into then contemporary technical work in mathematics and physics as well as empiricist sociology.

The case of Schlick as potential leader of a school is the more interesting one. The manifesto always placed Schlick first among equals. The manifesto was written for Schlick and Schlick was the center of the Circle, but it was the Vienna Circle, not the Schlick Circle, and its existence as informal entity was not so much due to Schlick as the reason Schlick decided to stay. The manifesto states that when Schlick decided "after some vacillation" to stay in Vienna:

> For the first time it became clear to him and to us that there is such a thing as the "Vienna Circle" of the scientific world-conception, which continues to develop this mode of thought in a collaborative effort. This circle has no rigid organization; it consists of people who have the same basic scientific attitude. Here the individual endeavors to fit in, everyone emphasizes that which unites, and no one wishes to disturb idiosyncratically the cohesion of the group. (Neurath et al. [1929] 2012, p. 77)

For his part and as we have seen, Schlick, when called upon to write a programmatic lead essay in the first issue of *Erkenntnis*, the new house journal of logical empiricism, in 1930, also stressed the adoption of a universal and scientifically acceptable method as the key to the new project in philosophy that the journal endeavored to promote. This, for Schlick, was, as the title of the essay indicated, a "turning point" in philosophy, and indeed precisely a turning away from schools and thus from "the fruitless conflict of systems" (Schlick [1930] 1959, p. 54).

The point of emphasizing the programmatic commitment of logical empiricism to scientific philosophy is not to say that the logical empiricists, by and large, were not committed also to logical analysis or to positivism or to empiricism. It is to say that notions like positivism, empiricism, and, indeed, logic were themselves taken by many of the logical empiricists to be obscure philosophical terms that needed, as an element of philosophy becoming scientific, to be given a clear meaning or, should that not be possible, to be set aside. "Science" was not, however, an obscure philosophical term – it was a term of everyday usage and what disciplines were sciences in the strictest sense could be fairly easily agreed upon. Moreover, although exactly how those sciences achieved their epistemic success was an epistemological question for logical empiricism, that those sciences had achieved such successes could be, so the logical empiricists believed, taken for granted – those practices could only be understood internally in a suitably scientific logic or philosophy of science. So it was a presupposition of the program that the sciences of physics and mathematics had achieved an unparalleled level of epistemic success and thus, to become scientific, philosophy should emulate them somehow. On the methodological front, analysis was not promoted simply because it was analysis, but because the status of logic as the framework within which formalized science was already being done. There could be no doubt that logical analysis occurred in the exact sciences. Hilbertian axiomatization of geometry, the Frege–Russell reduction of mathematics to logic, Einstein's account of simultaneity of events at a distance – all of these were understood to be logical analyses within the exact sciences. "Analysis" itself, especially if modified with a philosophical term like "epistemological" and contrasted with "psychological," would need some clearing up.[17] But, among the reasons why the exact sciences were exact was that they dealt with precise concepts and they did so as a result of logical analysis – this too was presupposed and thematized in the work of the logical empiricists.

Emphasizing this programmatic commitment does not reintroduce a false interpretative unanimity among the logical empiricists. After all, the commitment is at such a high level that disagreements could – and did – break out at any of several different points. The logical empiricists disagreed about how to account for the success of the exact sciences themselves. They disagreed about the nature of analysis and about the range of application of the formal tools of logic. They disagreed about the properly scientific replacement of empiricist epistemology and about the relation of that project to psychology. They disagreed about how precisely to reject metaphysics and about what exactly was rejected when one did. They disagreed over the very term "scientific philosophy," which was one of many terms Neurath unequivocally rejected (since it did, after all, include the word "philosophy"). But stressing the joint commitment to making philosophy scientific both allows these disagreements to be structured in an illuminating way and indicates how the disagreements neither proceeded without limit nor needed to disrupt the unity of the movement. This is because the commitment to scientific philosophy amounted to a commitment to certain norms of philosophical activity and to the use of certain methods and tools in philosophical research. As the manifesto stated: "The scientific world-conception is characterized not so much by theses of its own, but rather by its basic attitude, its points of view and direction of research" (Neurath et al. [1929] 2012, p. 81).

There are many questions, therefore, that a mere commitment to making philosophy scientific does not answer but that any version of scientific philosophy must ultimately decide upon. If philosophy is to be one science among

---

[17] This is Carnap's chief task in his *Pseudoproblems in Philosophy* (Carnap [1928] 1961b).

many, then presumably it differs from other sciences in virtue of its topic, its objects of study. What, then, is the proper topic of scientific philosophy? What methods are appropriate to a science with such a topic and what vouchsafes the scientific status of such a method? Also, there are the issues involved with any attempt radically to reform a field of human intellectual endeavor – how can we vouchsafe that a philosophy made scientific is still properly philosophy? The scientific philosophy of the logical empiricists had answers to all these questions, answers on which there was broad but not full agreement among the logical empiricists. We shall examine their answers beginning in the final portion of this section, but first we must examine another virtue that interpreting logical empiricism as an episode in scientific philosophy has: the scientific status of philosophy was an important metaphilosophical issue in German and Austrian academic philosophy for about three-quarters of a century before the announcement of the logical empiricist version of scientific philosophy. Moreover, the issue had come pointedly to a head in the critical cultural climate of the period after World War I in the defeated German-speaking lands. We shall look at just one other example of this dynamic.

Scientific Philosophy in Germany and Austria in the Twentieth Century

There is a history that goes right through to at least the middle of the nineteenth century of concerns about the *Wissenschaftlichkeit* of philosophy within the German and Austrian philosophical communities. This history is long and complicated. It involves varying sensibilities about what *Wissenschaftlichkeit* is, what virtues a scientific philosophy would have and what vices it would avoid, what alternative models for philosophy and philosophical activity there are, and so on. We clearly do not have the space or patience for much of that history here. But it is useful briefly to cover some aspects of the issues as they were discussed more widely within the generation from which the nascent logical empiricists learned philosophy and among some of their prominent contemporaries.[18]

In the generation before the rise of logical empiricism, German scientific philosophy had many varieties, including the positivism of Ernst Mach and Richard Avenarius, various neo-Kantianisms but especially those advanced by the Marburg school, and the sociological empiricism of Ferdinand Tönnies. But, in the years just before World War I, perhaps the most important call for scientific philosophy came from Husserl on behalf of phenomenology.

---

[18] More details are in Richardson (1997); here I use some of the same material to a somewhat different end.

In 1911, Husserl wrote an long essay for the journal *Logos* entitled "Philosophie als strenge Wissenschaft [Philosophy As Rigorous Science]" (Husserl [1911] 1965). Husserl too attacked the lack of scientific credibility of philosophical systems hitherto. This leads immediately to a question: "For with this blunt emphasis on the unscientific character [*Unwissenschaftlichkeit*] of all prior philosophy, the question immediately arises whether philosophy is to continue envisioning the goal of being a rigorous science, whether it can or must want to be so" (Husserl [1911] 1965, p. 65). Husserl's answer is that philosophy must be a science if it is to be anything at all. He too lays much of the blame for its lack of scientific credibility on a mistaken notion of philosophical genius, leading to systems that ultimately are kept in a "silent museum of history" instead of providing a foundation for future philosophical work. To rectify this, there needs to be a reorientation of philosophical understanding of the epistemic virtues of the philosopher, who, says Husserl, works in an "impersonal" science and thus needs "not wisdom, but theoretical talent" (Husserl [1911] 1965, p. 149).

Husserl's chief contribution to scientific philosophy is not the originality of the arguments he deploys against earlier *unwissenschaftliche* philosophy. It is, rather, in his enunciation of a radical alternative vision of what science philosophy properly was. Husserl insisted that phenomenology was so new that most philosophers had no concept of it. And what was phenomenology? It was a science of pure consciousness:

> A science of consciousness that is still not psychology, a phenomenology of consciousness as opposed to a natural science about consciousness … Psychology is concerned with "empirical consciousness," with consciousness from the empirical point of view, as empirical being in the ensemble of nature, whereas phenomenology is concerned with "pure" consciousness. (Husserl [1911] 1965, p. 91)

Husserl's job as a phenomenologist, then, was both to clarify what this "pure consciousness" is and to develop methods appropriate to a science of it. Indeed, these methods are the best way to develop the account of pure consciousness, since pure consciousness is revealed in and through the method of *epoché*, which allows the bracketing of content of mental activity and the revealing of the pure act. We cannot develop the account of phenomenology in any detail here. What matters in this context is the clarity of Husserl's insistence that phenomenology was scientific, indeed rigorously so. He too offered his new account of the project of philosophy as a way to introduce scientifically acceptable methods into philosophy and to achieve scientifically respectable results in philosophy.

The defeat of the German and Austrian empires in World War I induced a deep cultural, intellectual crisis in those countries. There was an important reaction against what was understood to be a pristine and ultimately failed reliance on rationality in the German-speaking world. Oswald Spengler's *The Decline of the West* (Spengler [1918/1922] 1991) was only the most successful of a series of attacks on the scientific culture of Germany. These attacks led to the rise in metaphysical and theological thinking to which we have already seen the logical empiricists, in the late 1920s, giving attention; it was also the reason for the flowering of *Lebensphilosophie*. Among its many consequences, the new era led to a radical reformation of phenomenology as Heidegger repudiated Husserl's insistence that phenomenology was scientific philosophy.

Throughout the 1920s, Heidegger often explained his philosophical work by relating it to science. For example, Heidegger began his 1925 lecture course at Marburg with a lengthy discussion of the movement of scientific philosophy. In this history, he gives pride of place to phenomenology and thus to the figures of Franz Brentano, Wilhelm Dilthey, and Husserl. But the way he expresses himself also shows clear debts to the neo-Kantians with whom he had studied. The following long quotation gives a clear sense of the newness and promise of scientific philosophy – and indicates how he saw his own work as within this tradition:

> To summarize: In the middle of the nineteenth century a well-defined scientific philosophy gained prevalence. The expression "scientific philosophy" has a threefold sense. This philosophy characterized itself as scientific:
>
> 1. Because it is a philosophy of the sciences, that is, because it is a theory of scientific knowledge, because it has as its actual object the fact of science.
> 2. Because by way of this inquiry into the structure of already given science it secures its own theme that it investigates in accordance with its own method, while it itself no longer lapses into the domain of reflection characteristic of the particular sciences. It is "scientific" because it acquires its own domain and its own method. At the same time, the method maintains its security by its constant orientation to the factual content of the sciences themselves. Speculation aimed at world views is thereby avoided.
> 3. Because it seeks to give a foundation to the various disciplines that are directed toward consciousness through an original science of consciousness itself, a *psychology*. (Heidegger [1925] 1985, pp. 18–19)

By placing his work within a tradition of scientific philosophy only extant since the middle of the nineteenth century, Heidegger was able to thematize philosophically the fact of science and offer a version of a phenomenology of consciousness. His work also reacted against the speculative excesses that damaged philosophy's scientific credibility.

All this began to change after *Being and Time* was published in 1927. As he moved from phenomenology to fundamental ontology, Heidegger also readopted the older understanding of science as a systematic body of knowledge – precisely what Husserl's insistence on *strenge Wissenschaftlichkeit* was meant to indicate was not sufficient. Thus Heidegger argued in his *Basic Problems of Phenomenology* that there was nothing of real interest in scientific philosophy, since "that philosophy is scientific is implied by its very concept" (Heidegger [1927] 1982, p. 12). Indeed, philosophy has always and everywhere attempted to be science, indeed a particular science, ontology: "It can be shown historically that at bottom all the great philosophies since antiquity more or less explicitly took themselves to be, and as such sought to be, ontology" (Heidegger [1929] 1982, p. 12). Only by adopting a broad and ancient notion of science – not the notion of science that the scientific philosophers contrasted with the merely systematic and that thus made the scientific status of philosophy worth arguing about – could Heidegger hope to pull off the feat of demonstrating that all the great philosophies sought to be a science of being. Indeed, although Heidegger continued to use the phrase "*wissenschaftliche Philosophie*" in the introductory sections of *Basic Problems*, he argued that the phrase was redundant; scientific philosophy was simply philosophy per se. In his *Einleitung in die Philosophie*, a collection of lecture notes from 1928 to 1929 at Freiburg, he analogized the term "scientific philosophy" to the term "round circle," a simple spelling out of a concept (Heidegger [1928/1929] 1996, pp. 16–18).

As the point of contention motivating the scientific philosophers, including Husserl and Heidegger's own younger self, began to slip away, ontology or metaphysics began, in Heidegger's work, to show something more: metaphysics indicates the way in which philosophy goes deeper than mere science. By raising the problem of *Dasein* and its relations to Nothing, metaphysics passes beyond all special scientific rigor. Metaphysics raises the existential question of being; metaphysics is authentic existence. As he writes in his 1929 essay, "Was ist Metaphysik?": "No amount of scientific rigor attains to the seriousness of metaphysics. Philosophy can never be measured by the standard of the idea of science" (Heidegger [1929] 1977, p. 112). Phenomenology had become entirely philosophically inverted – having begun as a way to secure the strictly scientific nature of philosophy, it had, in Heidegger's hands, by 1930, instead been used to show that philosophy was intrinsically other and more serious than exact science.[19]

---

[19] I am not the person to explain in detail the reasons for the changes in Heidegger's philosophical views on science and philosophy. Within the context of his relations to logical empiricism, especially Carnap, see Friedman (2000a) and Stone (2006).

Scientific Philosophy and Analytic Philosophy

The range of German and Austrian scientific philosophies, including versions of empiricism, neo-Kantianism, and phenomenology (and the list could be extended), reaches well beyond the scope of what we now consider to be the founders, in the German context, of analytic philosophy. Indeed, Gottlob Frege, the German "founder" of analytic philosophy par excellence, who was a mathematician, did not have well-worked-out views on the scientific status of philosophy. The intellectual status of philosophy was not a major concern of his.

It is of interest, though, that of the three "leading representatives of the scientific world conception" listed at the end of the *Wissenschaftliche Weltauffassung*, two were Bertrand Russell and Ludwig Wittgenstein (Neurath et al. [1929] 2012, pp. 108–111). (The third was Albert Einstein.) The case of Wittgenstein is, as one might expect, vexed. It is hard to read various pronouncements of the one published piece of philosophy he had published by 1929 – his *Tractatus Logico-Philosophicus* – as calling for a scientific philosophy. Indeed, one might well think that the case for Wittgenstein as scientific philosopher is ruled out explicitly in 4.111, when Wittgenstein writes, simply enough: "Philosophy is not one of the natural sciences. (The word 'philosophy' must mean something whose place is above or below the natural sciences, but not beside them.)" (Wittgenstein [1921] 2001)

Wittgenstein's use of the term "natural sciences" here should not mislead us. He is not saying or suggesting that philosophy is a social or cognitive science. Indeed, in 4.1121, he says as much regarding psychology, which he is happy to call a natural science: "Psychology is no more closely related to philosophy than any other natural science."

Nothing about Wittgenstein or his relationship to the Vienna Circle is simple, however, and between these two statements, Wittgenstein endorses a view that becomes a central component of the scientific philosophy that the logical empiricists endorsed. What is not clear is whether this view is an endorsement of scientific philosophy in Wittgenstein's own work:

> 4.1121 Philosophy aims at the logical clarification of thoughts.
> Philosophy is not a body of doctrine but an activity.
> A philosophical work consists essentially of elucidations.
> Philosophy does not result in "philosophical propositions," but rather in the clarification of propositions.
> Without philosophy thoughts are, as it were, cloudy and indistinct: its task is to make them clear and to give them sharp boundaries. (Wittgenstein ([1921] 2001)

In some versions of logical empiricism from the late 1920s onward, this account of philosophy is substantially endorsed. In logical empiricism, this is a way of making philosophy scientific – philosophy becomes a logical method of clarifying propositions, which all properly belong to science. Philosophy is the process of clarifying the propositions of science and of distinguishing them from the pseudo-propositions of metaphysics; it is not the science of another realm of properly philosophical objects or facts. The result of logical analysis is then a fully clarified science and nothing else – but this process is already to be seen in scientific work; philosophy extends scientific work in this way. In the very process of clarification, the pseudo-problems of metaphysics drop out. This seems to be the position of Wittgenstein's antepenultimate section:

> 6.53 The correct method of philosophy would really be the following: to say nothing except what can be said, i.e. propositions of natural science – i.e. something that has nothing to do with philosophy – and then, whenever someone else wanted to say something metaphysical, to show him that he had failed to give a meaning to certain signs in his propositions. Although it would not be satisfying to the other person – he would not have the feeling that we were teaching him philosophy – *this* method would be the one strictly correct one. (Wittgenstein [1921] 2001)

While we cannot hope to unravel all the mysteries of Wittgenstein's text, the question regarding his own understanding of such claims and how the logical empiricists understood them reduces, one might say, to what "has nothing to do with philosophy" means here. For the logical empiricists, it is clear that all that can be said is the propositions of science and there is no additional field called philosophy that offers more propositions about its own realm of objects. Wittgenstein's views invite, especially in light of his discussions of the "unsayable" or "the mystical" at the end of the *Tractatus*, an interpretation that there is something beyond, in some sense, what can be said in science. This beyond can be gestured at or pointed to – shown – in philosophy and it is more important than the limits of what can be said. Just before 6.53, for example, Wittgenstein writes this in 6.522: "There are, indeed, things that cannot be put into words. They *make themselves manifest*. They are what is mystical." All this seems antithetical to logical empiricism.

Whatever Wittgenstein's ultimate disposition in matters pertaining to scientific philosophy, one founder of analytic philosophy who is central to the vision of philosophy in logical empiricism and who did advocate, unequivocally, for scientific philosophy was Bertrand Russell. The complete title of his 1914 Lowell Lectures was *Our Knowledge of the External World As a Field for Scientific Method in Philosophy* (Russell [1914] 1993). As the title indicates, the main object of the book was to illustrate how a philosophy using a properly scientific method would look; the problem of our knowledge of a world external to our minds is one topic to which that method is applied, but it is illustrated via other topics such as infinity and continuity and causation and free will. The properly scientific method for philosophy on offer in the book is the "logical-analytical method in philosophy." This method he assigns to Frege as the founder, and it is best exemplified, of course, in the enormous work he and Alfred North Whitehead did in attempting to extend Frege's work and derive all of mathematics from the principles of logic.

Throughout the book, Russell was insistent that this new method is but the scientific method applied to logic conceived as a science of the possible. He too despairs of progress in philosophy in the absence of a generally agreed-upon method for achieving solid results. He ascribes the particular crisis of intellectual authority that philosophy is suffering in the early twentieth century to the "stupid and trivial" logical errors of Hegel and Hegel's malign influence on British philosophy, especially F. H. Bradley. But he expands the list of nonscientific philosophy to include, importantly, the evolutionism of Friedrich Nietzsche, Henri Bergson, and Herbert Spencer. These philosophers are perhaps even more anti-scientific than Hegel, who was simply a poor logician. Nietzsche, Bergson, and Spencer are accused of intellectual dishonesty: they aimed to write philosophies not as dispassionate exercises in truth but in order to fulfill their own moral wishes. This violates the proper attitude of the seeker after truth, on Russell's view, and confuses the issue of passing judgment upon the world with the issue of understanding the world. For Russell, a proper scientific attitude is necessary for philosophy to progress and thus ethical neutrality is the first step to a properly disinterested approach to philosophical matters. A scientific philosophy must not presume to speak directly to practical issues of humanity:

> The philosophy, therefore, which is to be genuinely inspired by the scientific spirit, must deal with somewhat dry and abstract matters, and must not hope to find an answer to the practical problems of life. To those who wish to understand much of what has in the past been most difficult and obscure in the constitution of the universe, it has great rewards to offer – triumphs as note-worthy as those of Newton and Darwin, and as important, in the long run, for the moulding of our mental habits. And it brings with it – as a new and powerful method of investigation always does – a sense of power and a hope of progress. Many hopes which inspired philosophers in the past it cannot claim to fulfil; but other hopes, more purely intellectual, it can satisfy more fully than former ages could have deemed possible for human minds. (Russell [1914] 1993, pp. 40–41)

A scientific attitude gets one part of the way toward a science, but not all of the way. For Russell, the key to scientific philosophy, as we have noted, is the methods of the new logic, applied to whatever subject matter. Indeed, because logic is absolutely general, for Russell, the logico-analytic method is applicable to any subject matter. He illustrates the power of the new logic, for example, by considering how simply understanding that there are relations (such as betweenness of points) that hold not among two but among three or more entities can transform the understanding of cognitive states. Belief, for example, need not be a relation between a mind and a fact or state of affairs believed. After all, what of false beliefs, where there is not object in the world corresponding to the content of the belief? If we see belief as a many-place relation between a mind and various entities (including logical entities) that can form a proposition, such paradoxes can be relieved. With a new method in hand, philosophy can advance beyond a clash of attitudes and opinions: "The new logic provides a method which enables us to obtain results that do not merely embody personal idiosyncrasies, but must command the assent of all those who are competent to form an opinion" (Russell [1914] 1993, p. 69). The book rings with a modernist spirit, with philosophy called to align itself with the rational and scientific in opposition to the merely tradition and literary:

> Of the prospect of progress in philosophy, it would be rash to speak with confidence. Many of the traditional problems of philosophy, perhaps most of those which have interested a wider circle than that of technical students, do not appear to be soluble by scientific methods . . . The one and only condition, I believe, which is necessary in order to secure for philosophy in the near future an achievement surpassing all that has hitherto been accomplished by philosophers, is the creation of a school of men with scientific training and philosophical interests, unhampered by the traditions of the past, and not misled by the literary methods of those who copy the ancients in all except their merits. (Russell [1914] 1993, pp. 245–246)

It is certainly possible to endorse analysis as a (or even the) method in philosophy without endorsing it as a scientific method. It is possible even to endorse the analytic method without finding the goal to make philosophy scientific an interesting, a worthwhile, or even a coherent one. It is, as we saw in the cases of Husserl and the other nonanalytic scientific philosophers, on the other hand, quite possible to endorse the goal of making philosophy scientific without endorsing the analytic method. Nonetheless, for both Russell and, following him, the logical empiricists, the endorsement of analysis as the method of philosophy was that this method allowed philosophy finally to become properly scientific.

Logical Empiricism As Scientific Philosophy

Logical empiricism on the view presented here formed a family of allied versions of scientific philosophy. It is now the time to specify further what family it was. To do this, we need to know more about its objects and methods of inquiry. It is not too much to say that the principal projects for enunciating a properly scientific philosophy for the logical empiricists was to find a way to endorse a suitably scientific version of an analytic method for philosophy, to avoid any remaining metaphysical impulses or consequences of such a method, and to employ the method primarily to illuminate the epistemology of the sciences. But their scientific philosophy goes well beyond the details of such efforts and includes informal sensibilities regarding the epistemic and social virtues of science and scientific philosophy. And, again, consistent with the literature on pluralism in logical empiricism, we need to be mindful of underlying disagreements while also attending to cooperation and agreement being part of the image of science by which the logical empiricists were possessed.

Husserl's vision of scientific philosophy was as an a priori science of pure consciousness; such a vision specifies an object (pure consciousness) as the topic of scientific philosophy and requires methods proper to that object. Moreover Husserl had to specify why those methods trained on that object yield knowledge properly considered scientific – how phenomenology would not become another historical monument to individual genius. (On that score, phenomenology has turned out not to have done so well.) At least this much is required of any vision of scientific philosophy, the scientific philosophy of the logical empiricists emphatically included. Moreover, if our focus on scientific philosophy is hermeneutically successful, then we should be able to organize the diversity of logical empiricism better under the general headings of scientific philosophy than we were under headings offered in the other accounts. The point is not to deny but to understand the diversity of logical empiricism when it is understood as scientific philosophy.

Now, while several logical empiricists had interests in phenomenology, logical empiricism was not a branch of phenomenology. Husserl's answers to the question of what made his project scientific philosophy get us nowhere in understanding logical empiricism. On the issue of the subject matter of scientific philosophy, logical empiricism cleaved much more closely to a view that had, by the late 1920s, been associated for decades already with both positivism and some forms of neo-Kantianism: philosophy was the science that took the form of science and the methods of science as its topics. The point was to both understand and adopt those methods. The most prominent trope of logical empiricist scientific philosophy was, in the end, methodological. What in the first instance guaranteed the scientific status of logical empiricist philosophy is the use of modern formal logic as the method of doing philosophy. Indeed, the methodological place of logic was not so much offered in an account of the special objects of philosophical concern as in the rejection of both such special objects and special ways of knowing them – logic and the rejection of metaphysics go hand in hand. We have already seen the way that the logical empiricists placed much of the burden of the crisis of intellectual authority of philosophy on an alleged set of extra-empirical objects and metaphysical methods for accessing those objects. The logical empiricists wished to reject endless, fruitless – because methodologically intractable – arguments about transcendent values or intuitive understandings of the very nature of things or philosophical posits such as things in themselves or the Absolute or the Nothing. Thus logical empiricism began, rhetorically, with a rejection of standard ways in which philosophers carved out their own special objects of study and methods of studying them. In this they expected their readership to share in the view that such efforts had failed and that this failure was exhibited in the stagnant nature of philosophy and was embarrassed by the progress of exact science.

In such arguments, the logical empiricists stressed neither the certainty nor the technical details of the new formal logic but rather its universality and inescapability.[20] It is here where the arguments of the logical empiricists look most like those of the neo-Kantians. Thus, for example, Carnap, in 1928, insisted that regimentation of any knowledge claims into strict logical form showed the ways in which alleged metaphysical claims lacked sense and meaning. But what grants to logic this role according to Carnap? It is guaranteed by logic's place as the sense-constituting framework of judgment. The basic concepts of logic are presupposed in science because they cannot properly be denied – denial is an act of judgment and judgment is only possible as judgment when logic is in place. For example, Carnap writes, "The concept of implication . . . is a fundamental concept of logic which cannot be criticized or even avoided by anyone: it is indispensable in any philosophy, nay, in any branch of science" (Carnap [1928] 1961b, p. 306).

In the case of Carnap in 1928, such claims show the influence of his teacher, Gottlob Frege. Frege had argued that the basic laws of logic formed the framework within which any judgment on any subject matter was first possible – to imagine a being using "different logic laws" is not to imagine a different type of judgment but a "hitherto unknown kind of madness" (Frege [1893] 1997, p. 203). But the influence of Bertrand Russell is also strong. As scouted earlier, much more vigorously than did Frege, Russell stressed both the centrality of logical analysis in philosophy and the scientific status of the philosophy so prosecuted.

For other logical empiricists in the late 1920s and early 1930s, similar sentiments owed more to Ludwig Wittgenstein. Thus, for example, Schlick's "Die Wende in die Philosophie" (Schlick [1930] 1959) makes a strong case that logical analysis is the only proper method in philosophy in ways both influenced by and strongly reminiscent of Wittgenstein's *Tractatus*, which Schlick

---

[20] This changes with the move to logical pluralism.

characterized as the final "push forward to the decisive turning point" in philosophy. Schlick assigns this decisive turning point to the understanding of the nature of logical truth in Wittgenstein, which he expresses this way:

> All possible modes of representation – if they otherwise actually express the same knowledge – must have something in common; and what is common to them is their logical form. So all knowledge is such only by virtue of its form. It is through its form that it represents the fact known. But the form cannot itself in turn be represented. It alone is concerned in cognition. (Schlick [1930] 1959, p. 55)

Carnap and Schlick had similar views circa 1930 of the nature of philosophy and the place of logic within it. Both believed that proper attention to the place of logic in philosophy decisively transforms epistemology by orienting it toward a logical investigation of the representation of knowledge claims. But Schlick's Wittgensteinian influence leads him to place great stress on the idea that philosophy is an activity, not a body of doctrine. For this reason, in "Wende," Schlick ultimately actually concludes that philosophy "is not a science" because it is not "a system of statements" (Schlick [1930] 1959, p. 56).

While this remark by Schlick might be understood as an embarrassment for the interpretation of logical empiricism on offer, I take it rather as the expression of tensions within the view of science and of logic, and thus of the scientific philosophy that logical empiricism offered, regarding which Schlick ends up at one extreme. Schlick's view of philosophy is an activity meant to show the meaning of scientific claims and the lack of meaning in metaphysical claims. Philosophy thus has no realm of objects proper to itself and thus no domain of truths of its own. If, then, a science consists of a set of truths about a domain of objects, philosophy in this sense cannot be a science. It is, however, an activity that participates in the clarificatory practices of the sciences and that serves the salutary purpose of distinguishing science from metaphysical nonsense. Moreover, it is an activity most evidently on offer within the sciences and that, when properly extended, could bring scientific rigor to any branch of inquiry. Schlick's philosophy is a scientific technology of clarification, not a body of doctrine; it is a scientific practice.

Philosophy ultimately, on this Schlickian view, rather disappears; the essay ends on this point:

> Philosophical writers will continue to discuss the old pseudo-questions. But in the end they will no longer be listened to; they will come to resemble actors who continue to play for some time before noticing that the audience has slowly departed. Then it will no longer be necessary to speak of "philosophical problems" for one will speak philosophically concerning all problems, that is: clearly and meaningfully. (Schlick [1930] 1959, p. 59)

When one recalls that the models of conceptual clarity that Schlick himself invoked were taken from the exact sciences, one can see that speaking "philosophically" amounts to speaking "scientifically." Philosophy is an activity in which exact scientists already fruitfully engage. Philosophy is not a science for Schlick ultimately because it disappears into the activities of science. Thus, while not a science in the strictest sense – not a body of doctrine on a specific subject matter – Schlick's philosophical method is motivated by conceptual work in the sciences, participates in the great intellectual virtues of such work (conceptual clarity, foremost), and is offered in aid of a scientific conception of the world.

Both of these accounts of the place of logic within logical empiricism can be described using a word common to Wittgenstein and Kant, "transcendental." Logic serves not as a body of doctrine about a specific subject matter, but as the precondition of the possibility of sense-making. To violate the rules of logic is not to say something false about the objects of logic, but to fail to say anything meaningful at all. A logic playing this transcendental function is a great boon to the attempt to overcome metaphysics, which can be shown to be nonsense precisely by being shown to violate the rules of logic. Metaphysics becomes "unsayable" in the sense that nothing that violates the rules of logic counts as a possible content of judgment at all. Of course, it was not just Wittgenstein who endorsed such a view before the logical empiricists did. It was a theme within the neo-Kantian tradition. Form is what renders content material for cognition. Such form cannot itself be questioned since any meaningful questioning presupposes that the form is in place. Moreover, with the collapse of Kantian pure intuition, such form was usually theorized as purely intellectual, as logical form. This was a project that all the logical empiricists could – and Carnap and Reichenbach explicitly did – associate with Cassirer's neo-Kantianism.[21] After making the metalogical turn, where Carnap departs from Schlick is in the thought that these features of logic preclude logic itself from being fully and explicitly capable of formulation – logical syntax provides the realm of precise, rigorous presentation of the logical forms of the various possible languages for science for Carnap.

The necessity of logic for any knowledge in any domain takes us only so far. As we have just noted, this is very much in accord with how logic was considered in neo-Kantianism also. One thing that distinguished logical empiricism from neo-Kantianism proper was the adoption of modern mathematical logic as logic. This provided the logical empiricists with a tool for engaging in

---

[21] For more on Cassirer's notion of the logical of objective knowledge, see Heis (2010) and Richardson (2016).

scientific philosophy that went well beyond the power of traditional logic and that had shown its clarificatory power already in the realm of mathematics in the work of Frege and Russell. It is quite clear in the work of Carnap, for example, that the primary example of the scientific work that could be done in the new philosophy was provided in the reduction of mathematics to logic in the project of logicism (Carnap [1922] 2019; [1928] 1961a, §2). For Carnap, this was less simply an exemplary achievement than the template and set of techniques for similar work in other fields. Carnap sought to exploit the techniques of explicit definition in Russell's language of *Principia Mathematica* to illuminate the conceptual relations of the sciences more generally. In his *Aufbau*, he presented this as a second branch of axiomatization of science – like Hilbert, we enunciate fundamental axioms, but we also provide a structure of explicit definitions to connect those axioms both to the experiential beginnings of knowledge and to other derived concepts and laws relating those derived concepts to one another in science.

An important change occurs in the 1930s as the logical empiricists, and, most systematically, Carnap, took up the metalogical point of view. Once we understand there to be many different logical systems each of which can be given its specific formal rules, the idea that there is one sense-conferring logical system no longer can be maintained. But Carnap still believed that sense was conferred internally to a logical system – only within a given logical system are there rules of inference and statements that convey the meanings of terms. Transcendent forms of necessity and universality were no longer the hallmarks of logical truth. Nonetheless, no question of, say, empirical justification for a claim could be made sense of if it was asked prior to and independently of a logical framework.

With this change in Carnap's views came a more explicit endorsement of a pragmatic and technological sense of the adoption of a logic. Metalogic offered "a boundless ocean of logical possibilities" and any one logical framework could only be chosen and adopted for practical reasons (Carnap [1934] 1937, p. xv). Among those reasons one could count ease of use for the purposes of formal or empirical science. Logical frameworks still did not answer to any framework transcendent question of accuracy – no such question could even be formed. Nonetheless, the commitment to adopting only a fully explicit formal language amounted to a form of intellectual honesty – since the consequences of such a choice could be investigated by all – and was modelled on the more local adoption of technical language in science.

A leading philosophical endeavor in the 1920s and 1930s of the wing of logical empiricism that dealt most intimately with physics was to use both the techniques of formal logic and the understanding of logic as a presupposition of sense-making (within a language) to bear on the issue of Einstein's achievement in physics. This is the topic of Carnap's 1922 dissertation, *Der Raum*, and various of his other writings throughout the 1920s. It was one of two principal foci of the early work of Reichenbach – the other was questions of the applicability of probability theory in physics – and led to a series of monographs right through 1928. It was the leading topic of his project in what he called *Erkenntnisanalyse* ("analysis of knowledge") or *Wissenschaftanalyse* ("analysis of science"). It was, even earlier, also important to Schlick's work and arguably gives the framework for his early master work, *General Theory of Knowledge* (Schlick [1918/1925] 1974). It was, as we saw in an earlier section, the setting within which Blumberg and Feigl (1931) introduced their American audience to logical empiricism.

In their later work, Reichenbach and Carnap sought importantly to generalize the themes they saw at work in Einstein and provide a generally conventionalist understanding of the language of science, indeed language generally. Carnap, in his later work, also explicitly took up the challenge of endorsing something like a Wittgensteinian model of logical truth while not resting content with a view that philosophical sentences are unsayable or elucidations or nonexistent. His *Logical Syntax of Language* explicitly sought to answer Wittgenstein on such matters, adopting a metalogical stance in which philosophical sentences are sentences about sentences. Philosophy became "the logical syntax of scientific language" or "the mathematics and physics of language" (Carnap [1934] 1937, p. 284). This in turn became the project of formal semantics. Training the techniques of metalogic on the languages of empirical science – to show how the logical frameworks offered the analysis or explication of even empirical terms and how notions like empirical justification were themselves best explicated in regimented languages with explicit formal logical rules – is Carnap's mature project in the logic of science.

Even among those logical empiricists interested in physics and mathematics, the details of logical empiricist scientific philosophy took somewhat different forms and had different emphases. Thus, for example, Philippe Frank's work was from the beginning less obviously concerned with formal logic and was more interested in historical and interpretative questions than was Carnap's. While endorsing the general line on the nature of scientific philosophy, Frank was mainly interested in freeing science from metaphysics in a more historical way, arguing that old scientific theories lived on as metaphysical dogmas that served to interpret current scientific theories in misleading ways. His point of view is expressed in these sentences from his *Encyclopedia* monograph:

> The lack of coherence in the presentation of a new physical theory often has its origin in the incoherence between the languages of the old and the new physical theories. The old language slips easily into the presentation of recent

physics. For it pretends to express a certain philosophy which is based upon intuition or good sense and cannot be disregarded by physicists. Actually this language has been invented to present older physical theories. It use means, therefore, confusing the language of recent physics with the language of older and abandoned theories. (Frank [1946] 1955, p. 428)

To combat this mode of interpretation of physics, Frank presented a different way of connecting the symbols of physics to the world, through the use of operational definitions. Consistent use of such definitions will overcome any sense of crisis in physics and connect the sentences of physics to the sentences of other sciences. Frank's project most clearly articulates with the centrality of formal logic exactly in his insistence that physical concepts as they appear in scientific laws are symbols that lack any inherent interpretation and thus do not in themselves provide evidence for any metaphysical doctrines. Thus, in the fight against mechanistic and idealist interpretations of science (the central concern of Frank's version of antimetaphysics), the purely symbolic nature of the scientific concepts plays a central role.

This emphasis on logic in logical empiricist scientific philosophy must confront the figure of Otto Neurath. Neurath has become well known for his naturalism, his interest in an empirical theory of science, and his skepticism with respect to the value of formal semantics in illuminating questions related to the unity of science. Thus, a joint project of scientific philosophy that focuses on the role of formal logic in specifying the genus of scientific philosophy logical empiricism would be troubled by Neurath's logical empiricism. And there can be no doubt that Neurath's unity of science project is not as easy to slot into this framework as those discussed earlier in this Element. Nonetheless, illumination comes from reading Neurath from this perspective.

We should note that the attempt to frame Neurath's philosophy in this way is not an external framework imposed on it from without. Repeatedly and especially in the 1930s unity-of-science project, Neurath framed his project this way: for him, the logical empiricist unity of science project married, as the titles of sections 4 through 6 of his "Unified Science As Encyclopedic Integration" indicated, an empirical scientific attitude that had been systematized in the modern era of science with the logical analysis of scientific statements (a project that for him was largely located in the nineteenth century with Leibnizean antecedents) into something he called "logico-empirical integration" (Neurath [1938] 1955). The resulting project resists easy summarizing but it is clear Neurath believed that logical analysis trained upon empirical science is an important part of it. Indeed, his use of the "the systematic analysis of 'planned economy'" indicates that he viewed some of his own work as this sort of logical analysis (Neurath [1938] 1995, p. 14).

This example, as well as some of the names Neurath mentions in discussing the history of logical analysis – such as Schroeder and Venn – indicates that perhaps Neurath's project is not so much anti-formalist or uninterested in modern logic as it is drawing from the resources of a different logical tradition from that associated with Frege and Russell, the tradition of algebraic logic. In a long and illuminating essay, Jordi Cat (2019) makes precisely this argument. Cat draws our attention to a series of early papers written jointly and individually by Neurath and Olga Hahn-Neurath that dealt with technical matters in the algebraic logic of Schroeder. Even more importantly, he shows that Neurath's work in the theory of economic planning is in the tradition of thinkers like Venn and Jevons, who used algebraic notions of calculation in economic theory while attempting to go beyond that work in ways informed by algebraic logic. Cat shows in detail how Neurath's concerns with topics in algebraic logic such as duality and univocality as well as the way algebraic logic showed how exact thinking could be obtain even in nonquantitative areas informed his economic work on economies in kind. On Cat's account, far from being a resistance fighter against logic in scientific philosophy, Neurath is more accurately described as deploying the resources of a different formal tradition in logic and using those resources to help explain the sort of nonquantitative calculation seen in the social sciences. Cat summarizes his view as follows:

> Moreover, adopting philosophical and historical perspectives to address broader or foundational questions, whether by Helmholtz, Mach, Schröder, Duhem, Poincaré or Neurath himself, [Neurath] seems gradually led by a twofold mistrust of naïve inductive empiricism and of speculative philosophy and by a commitment to a growing sense of scientific standards, closer to the disciplines that sought both foundation and reform, including the social sciences. Logic, partly in the image of mathematics, became the last scientific refuge of philosophy. (Cat 2019, p. 295)

Our outline here has been comprehensive neither in breadth nor depth. Space does not allow that. What I have hoped to provide is an initial plausibility argument that there is a fruitful reading of the work of at least these five figures central to logical empiricism – Carnap, Frank, Neurath, Reichenbach, and Schlick – in which their shared project was an effort to secure the scientific bona fides of philosophy, clarify some theretofore philosophical problems and set aside others, and to help in a broad project of aiding scientific advancement through their work in logical empiricist scientific philosophy. This reading illuminates their sense of a shared project despite myriad differences in both their commitment to specific philosophical doctrines and their sensibilities about the most important aspects of the scientific world conception.

Logical Empiricist Scientific Philosophy: Consequences and Legacies

We motivated our account of logical empiricist scientific philosophy in two ways. First, we noted things that are misleading or missing in the standard account of the significance of logical empiricism. Second, we stressed the importance of a unity to logical empiricism based more substantially on attitude, ethos, method, and goal than on the details of or commitment to specific doctrines. This is a short Element, and the riches of this new perspective on logical empiricism and its significance for twentieth-century philosophy can only be gestured at by attending to a few interpretative issues.

The issues we will cover briefly in this final section are these. First, we will provide a closer specification of the sort of scientific attitude or ethos embedded in logical empiricism and how that attitude informed how they did philosophy. For illustrative purposes in this section, we shall consider mainly Carnap's work and concentrate on his responses to Quine about the analytic/synthetic distinction. Second, we will look briefly at the political project or social function, if any, the logical empiricists vested in their philosophical work. For this section, we will use principally the work of Reichenbach to shed new light on a vexed issue in the interpretation of logical empiricism. The final topic returns to the question of how logical empiricism came to be understood as a chapter in analytic philosophy and seeks better to specify the question to which an answer still needs to be found and to outline a few factors that will have to be considered in a proper answer to the question.

The Ethos of Logical Empiricist Scientific Philosophy

As we have seen, the scientific turn in philosophy was not, for the logical empiricists, meant to be bound up with the details of doctrines and problems so much as it was with a spirit of properly scientific research. Such a spirit of research was given the name "the scientific ethos" by a sociologist of science contemporaneous with logical empiricism, Robert K. Merton, in the 1930s (Merton [1942] 1973). It is remarkable how well the Mertonian scientific ethos matches the informal sensibilities of the logical empiricists in the 1920s and 1930s. Attention to the scientific ethos of logical empiricism will give us a sense of the social organization of philosophical research that they advocated for as well as an indication of the epistemic value they invested in the project of making philosophy scientific.

The scientific ethos was one of Merton's most lasting contributions to sociology of science. It sought to explain the nature of the social cohesion of the scientific community by stressing a set of internalized norms used to regulate the behavior of those in the community. These norms are what is codified in the scientific ethos, which he glossed as follows:

> The ethos of science is that affectively toned complex of values and norms which is held to be binding on the man of science. The norms are expressed in the forms of prescriptions, proscriptions, preferences, and permissions. They are legitimatized in terms of institutional values. These imperatives, transmitted by precept and example and reinforced by sanctions are in varying degrees internalized by the scientist, thus fashioning his scientific conscience or, if one prefers, the latter day phrase, his superego. Although the ethos of science has not been codified, it can be inferred from the moral consensus of scientists as expressed in use and wont, in countless writings on the scientific spirit and in moral indignation directed toward contraventions of the ethos. (Merton [1942] 1973, pp. 268–269)

Merton's codification stressed four elements, bound together in the mnemonic device KUDOS, which stands for "communism" (later, "community"), "universalism," "disinterestedness," and "organized skepticism." Communism refers to the way in which scientists treat scientific research results as common intellectual property, not owned by the person who discovered them and not held in secret. Universalism refers to scientists' sense that science is not unique to one specific place, that its methods and results are applicable regardless of the location of the research, the ethnicity, gender, or other peculiarities of the scientists, and so forth. Disinterestedness refers to an institutional norm that enjoins scientists to set aside personal goals or interests in order to pursue scientific knowledge solely in the interest of the acquisition of knowledge. This norm is the reason, according to Merton, that "there is a virtual absence of fraud in the annals of science." Organized skepticism refers to the social face of a view of science most philosophers would associate with Karl Popper's (Popper [1963] 2002) view of science as an open society of criticism and severe testing of scientific claims – the scientific community organizes itself not as a community of belief but of skepticism. The proper response to a claimed scientific finding is critical and involves "the temporary suspension of judgment and the detached scrutiny of beliefs in terms of empirical and logical criteria" (Merton [1942] 1973, p. 277).

Merton's sociological perspective sought to use the scientific ethos to provide explanations of larger social aspects of the scientific community. Thus, for example, communism was meant not simply to explain why scientists do not typically keep their results a secret, but also to indicate the value they place on communication of results and also why the disputes that do arise are over not ownership of but credit for results. Thus, Merton claimed to have an explanation for things like priority disputes in science – a tool such as the calculus is made available to anyone who might wish to use it and what is left to fight over is the credit for the innovation itself. Moreover, the fierce nature of many priority disputes indicate that it is misplaced to ascribe to scientists a global disinterestedness or generosity of mind. Merton thought it was a mistake to try to assign a unique psychological makeup or particular moral virtue to individual scientists; their behavior was as much determined by the social structures of science as is the behavior of priests by the social structure of the church or professors by the social structure of academia.

Within the motivational literature of logical empiricism, these norms are continuously expressed. Universalism finds a very clear voice in the repeated insistence that the project of scientific philosophy is an international project and in the efforts to make it quite visibly an international effort. The text of the *Wissenschaftliche Weltauffassung* details efforts in Austria, Germany, France, Italy, the United States, and elsewhere within scientific philosophy and toward unified science. Moreover, the lists of those sympathetic to the Vienna Circle or of leading representatives of the scientific world conception include Germans, Britons, and Scandinavians. Neurath's encyclopedia was pointedly an *international* encyclopedia with members of the editorial board in Austria, Germany, the United States, Sweden, Turkey, Denmark, Italy, Poland, England, and France. In the text of his introductory essay, Neurath stresses the universal communicability of scientific knowledge, and does so, as is his wont, in the most ordinary examples:

> The empiricalization of daily life is increasing in all countries: cities in the United States and in Japan, highways in Mexico and Germany, armies in China and France, universities in Turkey and Italy – all show us certain common features. A meteorologist trained in Denmark may become a useful collaborator to a Canadian polar expedition; English economists can discuss a Russian analysis of American business cycles; and Russian economists may object to or accept the opinions of English economists about the effect of rural collectivization in the Soviet Union. (Neurath [1938] 1955, p. 22)

Especially as the 1930s progressed and European nationalism and fascism grew in strength, this rhetoric often became more explicit and more pointed. In 1936, Reichenbach, a German Jew relocated to Ataturk's modernized Istanbul after the racial purge of German universities, wrote in an American journal: "Science, surely, is not limited to national or racial boundaries; we prefer to stand for this historical truth, in spite of all pretensions of a certain modern nationalism. We therefore invite empiricists and logisticians of all the world to share in our discussions" (Reichenbach 1936, p. 160).

The norm of disinterestedness, meanwhile, can be read as being at the center of Carnap's rejection of metaphysics. In claiming that metaphysicians sought to provide a personal view of the world while dressing it in the language of theoretical knowledge, Carnap in essence accused them of confusing their personal desires and values with the doctrines of an intellectually responsible philosophy. His demand for justification of philosophical claims before a community of scientific coworkers indicated his alternative vision of philosophy, one quite clearly modeled on the workings, as he understood them, of the scientific community. It also exploited the view of the scientific community as embodying organized skepticism, since Carnap took for granted that the justificatory process within scientific philosophy would, because modeled on the scientific process, be onerous.

The point of noting the relations between Merton's ethos of science and the informal sensibilities about science implicit in the remarks of the logical empiricists is not to provide evidence that Mertonian sociology of science is timelessly correct about how science works. The point is, rather, that at the time when Merton was formulating his norms of science, those norms were widely endorsed and expressed by a group of philosophers aiming to induce scientific standards in philosophy. Merton was attuned to an element of his contemporary science important enough to have been central to the account of science exploited by those philosophers. At very least, then, there was a modernist moment in which the Mertonian ethos of science was mobilized sufficiently frequently and centrally for it to be at that time taken as an element of *Wissenchaftlichkeit* itself.

One of Merton's purposes in enunciating the ethos of science was to argue that science has a normative structure more in keeping with an open and democratic society than a closed fascist or other totalitarian society. The essay we have been quoting from was originally published in 1942 under the title "Science and Technology in a Democratic Order." Sensibilities about the affinity between a scientific philosophy and a democratic and generally socially progressive society were frequent in the literature of logical empiricism. We have seen it in Reichenbach's remarks on nationalism and in remarks in the *Wissenschaftliche Weltauffassung* on the relation of scientific philosophy and other progressive movements in social life. Several members of the Vienna Circle, as well as Reichenbach, in Berlin were clearly inclined to one or another form of democratic socialism during their younger years and right into the 1930s. Neurath was the most politically significant member of the Vienna Circle. He served in the short government of the Soviet Republic of Bavaria in 1919 and was helped out of jail through his contact with leading socialists in Red Vienna. Throughout his life, he worked on socially significant projects such as the ISOTYPE system for the visual representation of statistical information, which he used in various books and museum exhibits, in city planning, and many other activities. All these activities were in the service of getting a democratic polity to be able to deploy scientific findings in their policy choices.[22]

It is, moreover, clear that quite a bit of the impetus to reject metaphysics among the Vienna Circle members and in Berlin came from social concerns. Metaphysics was seen not simply as nonsense, but as a form of socially repressive nonsense, as stories that lacked meaning but served to prop up regimes of power and to obscure the true workings of the natural and social worlds. As the nods in the direction of the eighteenth-century French Encyclopedists served to indicate, this meant that logical empiricism had a sort of Enlightenment ambition in which the acquisition of reliable knowledge was understood as an intrinsic social good. Even more clearly, it aligned the logical empiricists with a modernist sensibility about the rationalization of social life, the promise of applied science, and the rejection of inherited but no longer pertinent social forms and roles. Vienna and Berlin were leading centers of progressive modernism in the German-speaking world during the interwar era; the scientific philosophy on offer from those centers was very much of a piece with this general tendency. This was reinforced also in the various joint projects the logical empiricists engaged in with groups like the Dessau Bauhaus and in the early adoption of new information technologies by, for example, Reichenbach, who appeared regularly on German radio to discuss science.[23]

Perhaps the way in which exclusive attention to theses or even to theses and methods in discussing logical empiricism is most inadequate is how much it underplays what we might call philosophical attitude as it is informed by the scientific ethos. Both in their motivational texts and, according to those they interacted with, the logical empiricists emphasized a philosophical approach that owed much to the attitude of scientists as they approached problems or questions. This attitude often impressed their students. Here is a characteristic account of her time as a graduate student of Reichenbach at the University of California–Los Angeles authored by Ruth Anna Putnam:

> He was an excellent teacher, of course; but he managed to do something which went beyond that. This was an undergraduate course and the material covered was not anything on which he was currently working; nevertheless he managed to give us the sense of participating in intellectual discovery. He did that partly by asking the right kinds of questions, questions which would force us to try to solve a problem before he presented the solution. But he did it also by telling stories, that is to say by making the situation in which the question would arise vividly real. (Putnam 1978, p. 62)

---

[22] See Cartwright et al. (1996) and Reisch (2005).

[23] On Enlightenment, see Uebel (2004) and Carus (2007); on modernism, see Richardson (2017, 2021).

Reichenbach, in his teaching practice, was of course trying to bring into philosophical training ways of approaching problems he had imbibed from his training in the sciences.

This attitude might seem to us unremarkable, but it was not so to American visitors to Germany and Austria in the late 1920s and early 1930s. In situ, logical empiricist philosophy and philosophical teaching was clearly an outlier. At the end of a witheringly funny critique of contemporary German philosophical obscurantism, Sidney Hook in 1930 made an exception for Reichenbach, to whose work he devoted the final few pages of the his paper; Hook found Reichenbach's special virtue as a philosopher opposed to the main currents of German philosophy to derive from his training in exact science:

> But the writings of the few German philosophers who have been trained in the exact sciences take a high place in the quality of German philosophical production. Of this group, Hans Reichenbach will probably be of most interest to the American reader. Ignored by academic philosophers as are all of his kind, his various works have won the praise of Einstein, Planck, and Russell. He himself is closely associated with men like Schlick, Carnap, and Grelling, although his position is more naturalistic than theirs. (Hook 1930, p. 159)

Similarly, Ernest Nagel, a few years later, found Schlick and Carnap notable for their pedagogical styles, styles they brought to philosophy from their scientific training (Nagel 1936).[24]

This philosophical style was not merely a matter of pedagogy (a vastly understudied area of philosophical history in its own right but one beyond our scope); it informed the research practice of the logical empiricists. Attention to this fact can allow us to see more clearly the philosophical importance of the shape of some of the controversies in which they were involved. To illustrate this fact, allow me to concentrate briefly on the famous dispute between Carnap and Quine on the analytic/synthetic distinction. Carnap was committed, as we have noted repeatedly, to an analytic/synthetic distinction and to the technical means necessary in semantics to draw the distinction rigorously in the case of formal languages for empirical science. Quine argued against this distinction.[25]

The question that will occupy us is not "who was right?" but rather "what was at stake in this dispute?" Quine had a consistent point of view on this question: the analytic/synthetic distinction was an important part of Carnap's commitment to

---

[24] We will return to Nagel (1936) in the next section.

[25] The central published documents of the debate are Quine (1951, 1963, 1969) and Carnap ([1950] 1956a, 1963, pp. 915–922), but the debate both depended upon Carnap's attempts to draw the distinction for formal languages right back to Carnap ([1934] 1937) and was prosecuted in private discussions and correspondence (see esp. Frost-Arnold [2013] and Creath [1991], esp. pp. 425–430).

empiricism. Carnap's strict empiricism was aimed at showing how the theoretical languages of science were meaningful by showing how those languages related to experience and it was, similarly, aimed at eliminating metaphysics by showing that metaphysical discourse could not be so related to experience. But Carnap was also committed to the meaningfulness and importance in the realm of knowledge of logic and mathematics. For this reason, Carnap needed a special account of the meaningfulness of logic and mathematics. He deployed the analytic/synthetic distinction to solve this problem: sentences of empirical science were synthetic; sentences of logic and mathematics were analytic. (Alleged sentences of metaphysics were not meaningful sentences at all.) He needed then to account for the meaningfulness of analytic sentences – this is what Quine dubbed "the linguistic doctrine of logical truth": analytic truths are true in virtue of the meanings of the words contained within them. For example, you only need to understand what "or" and "not" mean to know that "It is raining or it is not raining" is true.

Things get more complicated for the two types of sentence that are more important for systems of exact empirical knowledge: sentences of pure mathematics and sentences that provide the empirical meanings of scientific terms. We cannot go into all the complications, but the general idea is clear enough: some sentences, like "Bachelors are unmarried men," can be fairly straightforwardly read as stipulating the meanings of terms in an empirical language. You can try to extend this to include sentences that coordinate empirically known processes with mathematically well-defined notions like "straightest possible line" and come up with sentences like "Light rays are (I hereby stipulate by definition) (one class of) the straightest possible lines in space-time." But what of pure mathematics itself? Here the idea is basically to think of mathematics as based in axiom systems: take the axioms as constituting the meanings of the terms that occur within them; the theorems draw out the consequences of those implicit definitions. With these basic ideas, you can hope to preserve the proof procedures of pure mathematics as an epistemically illuminating activity and to indicate how systems of axioms so developed can be coordinated with experience, leading to rigorous and predictive sciences of nature.

Quine raises a number of objections to Carnap's attempts to make out an analytic/synthetic distinction. Quine concedes that if you presume there is such a distinction, there are myriad ways to make it out – truth by definition or convention, meaning postulates, and so on. But he finds all this reinterpretation unilluminating because none of these ways of making out the distinction answer the question an empiricist must answer: what empirical sense can we make of the distinction in the first place? We can raise this question in a number of different idioms: What empirical difference does labeling a set of sentences as "meaning postulates" or "stipulative definitions" make for the system of knowledge? Or, what behavioral difference for a language user maps onto to their holding a claim to be analytic rather than synthetic? Or, if we attend to how we actually learn language, what principled way of dividing our language into analytic and synthetic sentences is there? What, for example, would ground a claim that "this banana is yellow" is synthetic while "yellow is a color" is a conceptual, analytic claim about the type of property yellow is?

The poignancy of these questions stems from the fact that Carnap was, according to Quine, committed to the analytic/synthetic distinction as an empiricist. Because Quine could not find any empirical meaningfulness to the distinction, he deemed it ultimately an "unempirical dogma of empiricism" and offered a form of empiricism not committed to the distinction (Quine 1951). But Quine also came to realize in the course of the debate that Carnap found these arguments unpersuasive and beside the point. He began his 1963 paper by remarking on how difficult it is to raise objections to Carnap in terms Carnap accepts. Here I want to argue that this difficulty is not merely a further sign of Carnap's dogmatic insistence on the distinction. Indeed, for him, the analytic/synthetic distinction was not a part of his commitment to empiricism – it was rather a distinction that had to make sense for there to be an exact philosophy of the sort he wished to pursue to be possible at all. This meant that he did not in fact expect the analytic/synthetic distinction to be justified as Quine demanded or to bear the philosophical weight Quine alleged.

Signs of Carnap's puzzlement punctuate his responses to Quine. Carnap saw no reason why a semantic concept such as analyticity needs to be given a pragmatic criterion – nothing about the antecedent behavior of language users needs to map onto the semantic distinction between analytic and synthetic truths. He rejected the epistemological gloss ("held true come what may") that Quine places on analytic truths – he agreed with Quine that any sentence might be held true come what may but denied that this epistemological gloss captures the intent of the distinction in the first place. His frustration was apparent in his 1963 response to Quine where he adopted for one of the very few times in his publications a tone of humor or irony, essentially arguing that what Quine's work has shown was that for any given language the distinction between analytic and synthetic sentences was itself a logical distinction drawn in the semantic metalanguage and is not an empirical matter (Carnap 1963, p. 922). And this was of course the position Carnap himself endorsed.

We can see Carnap's point of view more clearly by looking at how he came to endorse empiricism. After his metalogical turn in 1930s, Carnap viewed empiricism as a proposal or a demand to use only certain languages in the reconstruction of science – empiricist languages that are delineated as such by a relationship (to be more fully filled out) between their synthetic sentences, and the protocol sentences that provide the empirical basis for science in that language (Carnap 1936/1937). But all of this presupposes the full apparatus of the logic of science: an array of languages in which an analytic/synthetic distinction has already been drawn, a delimitation of protocol sentences, and so on. Only with this structure in place is there even anything to propose adopting as the language of science. What empiricism in the twentieth century even could be for Carnap is a proposal or commitment within the technical project of the logic of science – empiricism presupposes rather than grounds a generally available analytic/synthetic distinction for formal languages.

It is for this reason that Carnap reverted at various times in his discussion to highly characteristic ways of speaking about his work and the place of analyticity within. In his response to Quine he wrote, for example, that "I believe that the distinction between analytic and synthetic statements, expressed in whatever terms, is practically indispensable for methodological and philosophical discussions" (Carnap 1963, p. 922). Similarly, the final paragraphs of his 1950 essay "Empiricism, Semantics, and Ontology" reveal what was at stake for him in the arguments against there being any meaning that can attach to the technical notions of semantics:

> The acceptance or rejection of abstract linguistic forms, just as the acceptance or rejection of any other linguistic forms in any branch of science, will finally be decided by their efficiency as instruments, the ratio of the results achieved to the amount and complexity of the efforts required. To decree dogmatic prohibitions of certain linguistic forms instead of testing them by their success or failure in practical use, is worse than futile; it is positively harmful because it may obstruct scientific progress. The history of science shows examples of such prohibitions based on prejudices deriving from religious, mythological, metaphysical, or other irrational sources, which slowed up the developments for shorter or longer periods of time. (Carnap [1950] 1956a, p. 221)

As we can see, the very progress of a science of philosophy was at stake for Carnap in these discussions. He was attempting to provide the technical tools for an exact science of philosophy and he saw in-principle arguments against the development of such tools as essentially equivalent to the irrational, metaphysical objections arrayed against the progress of science and the development of technical languages in science more generally. The analytic/synthetic distinction was a commitment within Carnap's vision of scientific philosophy because it was a component of a logic of science meant both to understand and to foster scientific progress.

Carnap's reversion in contexts such as these to speaking of semantics as providing instruments or tools was not merely coincidental. There is an important thread of the Carnap reappraisal scholarship that views him as engaged in a form of conceptual engineering.[26] The techniques of modern metalogic do not provide so much either a new set of problems for an empiricist to solve or a new set of techniques for an empiricist to deploy as it is a new, boundless set of languages for possible use in the clarification of whatever concepts we find philosophically unclear. For Carnap, one of those concepts was "empiricism" itself. This aspect of Carnap's philosophical perspective is having a bit of a renaissance – philosophy as conceptual engineering is in vogue in various corners of the philosophical world, although not necessarily in ways Carnap would recognize or endorse.[27]

This is not to dismiss Quine's concerns, of course. It is a call to attend to precisely what philosophical weight Carnap did and did not place on the distinction. Nor is it either to endorse conceptual engineering in general or in Carnap's specific version as a way forward in philosophy. But it does change the focus of the debate precisely to the ways in which the engineering metaphor can be pinned down to an actual working project and what the actual best practices within philosophical engineering would be. It also raises questions about whether "tools" like formalized languages are neutral with respect to what might reasonably be taken to be at stake in philosophical debates. But these are interesting and underdeveloped topics for a philosophical tradition that has not dropped all interest in technical projects; it is a worthy Carnapian legacy.

The Social Function of Logical Empiricist Scientific Philosophy

The question of practical reasons to choose specific logical frameworks for Carnap or indeed the decision to engage in science at all for Reichenbach is one entry point to another larger issue in the evaluation of the significance of logical empiricism. This is the issue of whether and, if so, in what sense logical empiricism, for all or at least some of its advocates, had a political project embedded within it. Our emphasis on logical empiricism as scientific philosophy both sharpens the issue and points to fundamental unclarities in much of the literature.

To sharpen the issue, let us recall first that in the early twentieth century, fairly generally and for the logical empiricists specifically, science was meant to be clearly distinguished from politics and from anyone's specific social interests. This is clear in the bits from Merton that we rehearsed. The norm of disinterestedness is specifically meant to dissuade scientists from deploying or advancing their special interests in their scientific work. This is a widespread understanding even today – for example, disclosure policies regarding financial contributions for

---

[26] See Creath (1990, 1991), Carus (2007), Richardson (2013), Brun (2016), and Dutilh Novaes (2020).

[27] See, for example, Cappelen (2018) and Isaac et al. (2022).

research and other conflict-of-interest mechanisms are standard parts of how science gets done. Beyond this general claim, the logical empiricists and several observers of their work in Europe understood the point of their scientific philosophy precisely to decouple the business of philosophy from the political and social roles that philosophy had been playing in Germany and Austria.

Among those who gave voice to such sentiments in what would turn out to be a poignant way was a young Nagel, in the 1936 essay briefly introduced earlier in this Element. Nagel reported on the rigor and the popularity of Schlick's teaching in Vienna. This clarity and rigor was an implicit rebuke not only by Schlick, but also by his students of the obscurantism of Germanophone philosophy and the dubious social and political purposes that philosophy was understood to underwrite. It is worth quoting Nagel at some length on Schlick's pedagogical presence:

> I did get a glimmer of insight into sociological motivations at Vienna. Professor Schlick's lectures were delivered in an enormous auditorium packed with students of both sexes, and in his seminar a stray visitor was lucky if he did not have to sit on the window sill. The content of the lectures, though elementary, was on a high level; it was concerned with expounding the theory of meaning as the mode of verifying propositions. It occurred to me that although I was in a city foundering economically, at a time when social reaction was in the saddle, the views presented so persuasively from the *Katheder* were a potent intellectual explosive. I wondered how much longer such doctrines would be tolerated in Vienna. And I thought I understood at least the partial reason for the vitality and appeal of analytic philosophy. Analytic philosophy is ethically neutral formally; its professors do not indoctrinate their students with dogmas as to life, religion, race, or society. But analytic philosophy is the exercise of intelligence in a special field, and if the way of intelligence becomes part of the habitual nature of men, no doctrines and no institutions are safe from critical reappraisals. Because traditional philosophy has so often been practised as a species of obscurantism, it has become the *bête noir* of the Wiener Kreis. (Nagel 1936, pp. 8–9)

Part of the poignancy of this quotation for us is precisely that Nagel was right to wonder how much longer Schlick's views would be tolerated in Vienna – about six months after Negal published this passage, Schlick was murdered on the steps of the University of Vienna. Whether his assailant was motivated by politics is a matter of some controversy, but there can be no doubt that his murder was celebrated in the protofascist right wing of Viennese intellectual life and the press.[28]

Nagel's take on the philosophical situation here is our current concern. Nagel makes clear two things: first, in his view, the techniques and doctrines Schlick taught were ethically neutral and, second, precisely due to this neutrality they

---

[28] A popular account of the Vienna Circle organized around the murder of Schlick is Edmonds (2020); Stadler (2015) reproduces many of historical documents relating to the event.

provided a potent tool against the political culture of Vienna. It was due to the political situation of mid-1930s Vienna that an ethically neutral philosophy could nonetheless have political value and valence. Here, then, is one way for a scientific philosophy to have political consequences: as a morally neutral source of philosophical techniques, it can provide tools to combat political structures built on philosophically obscure principles that sought to justify or at least explain social circumstances ("a city foundering economically") that a person might legitimately prefer to be otherwise. On Nagel's view, then, the political aspect of Schlick's philosophy was real, but contextual and contingent, not intrinsic to the project.

This is not everyone's take on at least certain versions of the logical empiricist project. In particular, those on the so-called left wing of the Vienna Circle – Neurath, Carnap, Hahn – are not infrequently said to have offered a form of scientific philosophy with an intrinsic political point. There is a robust literature arguing for and against such a view.[29] One feature of this literature is that disagreement about whether logical empiricism in any of its forms had an inherent political project embedded in it is often due to disagreement not about logical empiricism, but about what it means for an intellectual project to be political. This is, perhaps, unsurprising. As Mark Brown (2015) emphasizes, in discussions of the politics of intellectual life the word "politics" is an intrinsically contested term – there is no meaning for the term that is widely shared. So it is not surprising that this polysemy and vagueness creep into the literature on the politics of logical empiricism. A common tactic of analytic philosophy on such occasions is to stipulate a meaning for the term. No doubt there are situations in which this sort of stipulation is useful. Historical understanding of what the logical empiricists themselves thought about whether their philosophical projects were political is, however, not high on the list of intellectual tasks in which stipulating the meaning of "politics" as an analysts' term is useful. The interesting question is, rather, an historicist question – did any of the logical empiricists themselves have an understanding of "political" in which it could reasonably be said that their own project was political in their own sense?

This is not a question we can take up in detail with respect to any one logical empiricist, let alone the entire spectrum of them. But I think in short compass we can say a few things about one of the key figures that suggest the richness of the outlined approach. One of the logical empiricists whose early activist work required that he deploy a notion of the political was Hans Reichenbach. During

---

[29] Some of the key texts in this literature are Howard (2003), Reisch (2005), Uebel (2005, 2010, 2020), S. Richardson (2009a, 2009b), and Romizi (2012).

his student years, he was a political ideologist first for the *Freistudentenschaft* and then for the Student Socialist Party. In the former capacity, he wrote a 1913 essay on the goals of the *Freistudenten* movement in which he listed both educational and political goals that the group had.[30] He began his outline of the *Freistudenten* movement by enunciating a moral ideal to which the movement strived: "The supreme moral ideal is exemplified in the person who determines his own values freely and independently of others and who, as a member of society, demands this autonomy for all members and of all members" (Reichenbach [1913] 1978, p. 109).

With this in hand, he was able to specify two dimensions along which the movement made demands to reform the universities. The first dimension is educational. "Possibilities for education must be set up for the student; through lectures, chapter meetings, tours, and the like, the student must be offered opportunities to form his own judgments, to establish his own values. This is the Free Students' task with respect to *education*" (Reichenbach [1913] 1978, p. 111). But what is the Free Students' task "with respect to politics"? The overarching goal is to achieve "external conditions" that allow students to educate themselves toward the moral ideal. He specifies two aspects of achieving these external conditions: the first is freedom to teach and learn any subject matter, and the second is this: "To the extent that they are able, welfare agencies must combat the limitations possibilities for education under which students of limited means, who must earn their bread, suffer as result of social inequalities" (Reichenbach [1913] 1978, p. 111).

There is much of interest here, but our current concern is to use this understanding of the political – which has aspects both of liberty (freedom to teach and learn across subjects) and of economics (the reduction of the economic burdens on disadvantaged students) in support of the creation of autonomous individuals who fulfilled the moral ideal – to consider whether any aspect of it informs Reichenbach's subsequent work in philosophy of science proper. Here, we can only provide a brief sketch that indicates ways in which this structure of thinking does find expression also in his philosophical work. The main point is that Reichenbach's vision of the place of conventional decision in scientific knowledge indicates that science is a realm in which personal autonomy is expressed toward the end of a community-wide acquisition of knowledge. That is, conventions are freely chosen but are chosen with a community goal in mind, the advance of reliable, predictive knowledge.

---

[30] A broader consideration of Reichenbach's views on pedagogy and freedom can be found in Padovani (2021).

While this aspect of his account of politics stems from some of Reichenbach's early work, he returned again and again in his more popular, less technical writings to insist on this lesson from twentieth-century science: science is a realm of autonomy of thought and value in which the place of decision indicates that traditional Kantian understandings of the a priori were decisively rejected. This was an explicitly liberating thought for Reichenbach – Kant's chief flaw was to view both speculative and practical reason as rigid, permanent structures. This philosophical view had been decisively overthrown in the progress of science and should be decisively overthrown in the understanding of society. In the fractious interwar period, Reichenbach returned repeatedly to this lesson. In "The Philosophical Significance of Modern Physics" in 1930, for example, he puts the point this way:

> The collapse of traditional emotional values constitutes today the problem of life for every one of us, for every-day life, and although the revolution in physical science may have had its source in logical critique, its result is simply that science has taken its place in a sociological trend of our times. The caving in of the system of a priori categories and its replacement through the sober principle of induction, through the postulate of predictability, mirrors with utmost clarity the experiential situations of daily life; the same battles between outdated doctrine and new experiences are waged in both arenas. (Reichenbach [1930] 1978, p. 322)

This idea that a proper understanding of the revolutionary science of the twentieth century is a tool for the liberation of humanity from unjustified and unjustifiable systems of intellectual authority persists to the very end of Reichenbach's career. The final book he saw into print in his lifetime, the aptly named *The Rise of Scientific Philosophy* (Reichnbach 1951), returns to this theme in chapter 17 on the nature of ethics. There, Reichenbach wished to argue for an historically and socially contingent metaethical principle that he calls "the democratic principle": "Everyone is entitled to set up his own moral imperatives and to demand that everyone follow those imperatives" (Reichenbach 1951, p. 295). Of course, if it is a pluralist society, different individuals will have different moral imperatives and demands that cannot be fully rationally adjudicated. But Reichenbach simply believed that is how modern democratic societies work – that is not a problem for philosophy to try to overcome; that is the fact of our social lives.

The important point here is that Reichenbach finds this discussion a natural extension of the lessons of scientific philosophy. In neither the scientific nor the moral realm are there demands of reason that must be acceded to because as demands of reason they are binding on everyone. Instead, in both the realms of knowledge and of action, volitional decisions are offered for practical reasons and negotiated in the relevant public sphere. Reichenbach wants his readers to overcome any yearning they might have for anything more – the immutable demands of reason – and rather to participate with open eyes in the conciliation of volitions. Here's how he sums up his discussion:

> We try to pursue our volitional end, not with the fanaticism of the prophet of an absolute truth, but with the firmness of the man who trusts his own will. We do not know whether we shall reach our aim. Like the problem of a prediction of the future, the problem of moral action cannot be solved by the construction of rules that guarantee success. There are no such rules. (Reichenbach 1951, p. 301)

Is this account a "political project" for Reichenbach? Well, it continues along the lines of the first dimension of his 1913 account of the political project of the Free Student Movement – the autonomous individuals participating in the consilience of volitions need to be able to articulate their own volitional demands and to participate in social persuasion. The economic part of the political demands of the Free Students Movement is at least not explicitly brought up by Reichenbach and whether he has dropped this, the most socialist portion of his youthful political project, is not clear from the text. Would the Reichenbach of 1951 say that the project of this chapter is political? I conjecture that the answer would be no; this project is not so much part of the negotiation of volitional demands as it is a preliminary brush clearing so that the political life of contemporary democracy could move forward in full self-awareness; it is a propaedeutic to effective politics, perhaps. But if, with Brown, we see "politics" as an always contested notion, then the fact that a project is properly a protopolitical or metapolitical project does not mean it is not also a political project. It is, after all, an intervention in our culture's understanding of politics.

But it might perhaps be helpful to drop the contested term "political" as an analysts' or an actors' category. This is because what is often at stake in these discussions is actually rather incontestable except for vexation over whether this means logical empiricism was "political." That is, there can be no doubt that the fervor the logical empiricists brought to their projects and the tenor of documents like the 1929 manifesto or the preface to the first issue of *Erkenntnis* was due in part to their seeing a new, modernist, progressive social function for philosophy. Perhaps all social functions are political functions, perhaps not. It is not clear how critical it is to answer that question. In analogizing their philosophical project to modern architecture or new approaches to education, the Vienna Circle authors of the manifesto were certainly distinguishing the social function of scientific philosophy from that of obscurantist metaphysical philosophy. The advertisement for the Ernst Mach Society was explicit on this point – they were developing the tools of "modern empiricism . . . tools that are needed also in shaping public and private life" (Neurath et al. [1929] 2012, p. 112).

Carnap maintained this position throughout his career. Carnap considered the theses and methods of science as not themselves political but as scientific work that had positive social effects. In his response to Robert S. Cohen in the Schilpp volume, Carnap is explicit on this point:

> The theoretical theses of logical empiricism, based on analyses of procedures of knowledge and of the structure of languages and conceptual frameworks, are as such neutral with respect to possible forms of organization of society and economics. Nevertheless, even these theses have an indirect social effect. They give support to the view that strictly scientific methods are applicable also to the investigation of men, groups, and societies, and thereby they help to strengthen that attitude which is a precondition for the development of more reasonable forms of social order, forms in which the dehumanizing effects of the present organization of industrialization can be overcome. (Carnap 1963, pp. 865–866)

Historiography of Philosophy: Taking Scientific Philosophy Seriously

We shall end this reorientation of the interpretation of logical empiricism by briefly returning to a question left open earlier. The issue is how and why scientific philosophy became submerged in the understanding of the significance of logical empiricism and was replaced by "analytic philosophy." The discussion will not be complete or definitive, but rather suggestive of relevant facts and future directions of research.

First, let me be clear that the interpretation of logical empiricism as scientific philosophy, while not the only account of the project when it was received on American and British shores, was well represented in its early reception in North America. Scientific philosophy was the main point of agreement between the logical empiricists and perhaps the most important early American recruit to the project, Charles Morris. Morris wrote an essay in the 1935 volume of *Philosophy of Science* under the title "Philosophy of Science and Science of Philosophy," which begins: "It is proposed to examine the consequences which ensue if philosophy is deliberately oriented around the methods and results of science" (Morris 1935, p. 271). Having set himself that task, he examines, first, Carnap's proposal that philosophy is the logic of science and, second, the proposal he associates with Wittgenstein, Schlick, and Waismann that philosophy is the clarification of meaning. With respect to both of these conceptions, Morris objects that they threaten to lapse into empty formalism unless they are armed with a sufficiently general theory of meaning that can cover both the meanings of empirical and of formal claims. He argues that it is the pragmatist tradition, especially in the work of Peirce, that such a general semantics or semiotics can be found. It was this introduction of a Peircean tripartite distinction in the specification of the meanings of scientific claims that became Morris's most original contribution to scientific philosophy. In this essay, he introduces it as follows:

> Too much mystery is thrown around the analysis or clarification of meaning: the meaning of a term is completely specified when it is known what objects the term designates, what expectations it produces in the persons for whom it has meaning, and what its connections are with other terms in the language of which it is a part. The determination of the first gives the empirical dimension of meaning, the determination of the second gives the pragmatic dimension of meaning, and the determination of the third gives the formal dimension of meaning. (Morris 1935, p. 278)

The introduction of a formal pragmatics of scientific language was for Morris necessary to account for all dimensions of scientific meaning and his key corrective to Carnapian logic of science.

Morris continues the essay by discussing two more options for a scientific philosophy – empirical axiology, which he considers in Schlickian and Deweyan forms, and empirical cosmology. The latter he associates with Peirce, James, Dewey, Mead, and Whitehead; it is a form of empirical replacement for traditional metaphysics. In some ways, Dewey's version of the third conception is most central to Morris's own account, since Dewey's empirical axiology, per Morris, is an attempt to capture the scientific habit of mind or temper, which is very much continuous with Morris's own project. Our point, however, is quite simple: Morris viewed, correctly, both the Carnapian and Schlickian versions of logical empiricism as primarily attempts as bringing scientific methods and standards into philosophy, and he sought to advance that general project.

Another American philosopher of science who recognized and endorsed the scientific ambitions of Carnap's philosophy and who was at the time a more prominent philosopher was Curt Ducasse in his 1941 book *Philosophy As a Science* (Ducasse 1941). This book is mainly given over to three versions of scientific philosophy: Carnap's logic of science, an account of philosophy he tentatively associates with Dewey (and that he, interestingly, calls "philosophical engineering" (Ducasse 1941, p. ix)), and his own version. We do not have space to consider Ducasse's account of Carnap or his own version of scientific philosophy here, but his summary of his own project's relations to Carnap's project is worth noting. After briefly detailing the main features of Carnap's logic of science, Ducasse writes:

> Although I believe not only that Carnap does not prove these contentions but also that they are erroneous, I agree that *some* of the traditional problems of

philosophy are pseudo-problems. Accordingly, I believe that the attack of the logical positivists upon traditional philosophy has been salutary, for their demand for strictness of statement and for the credentials of the assertions one makes is tending to discourage the logically loose and empirically irresponsible sort of "philosophizing" which has only too often brought into disrepute the name of philosophy. (Ducasse 1941, p. ix)

Of course, one need not share the specific scientific ambitions of the logical empiricists to recognize that they had such ambitions for philosophy. In a lengthy, negative review of Reichenbach's *Rise*, Errol E. Harris argues that any philosophy capable of understanding scientific progress must be grounded in a form of logical metaphysics that he associates with Hegel. He ends his review with this assessment of Reichenbach's scientific philosophy:

> If we seek for scientific philosophy today, we must look for it in the works of the philosophers who followed Hegel in the classical tradition while they took into account and attempted to give philosophical interpretation of the results of modern science. This tradition leads to the names of such men as Bosanquet, Bergson, Alexander and Whitehead, whose work follows on those "systems of the nineteenth century" compared by Reichenbach to "the dead end of a river that after flowing through fertile lands finally dries out in the desert." The simile is tragically appropriate. The desert sands in which the river of philosophical thought is choked are the arid wastes of self-styled "scientific philosophy." (Harris 1952, p. 165)

Of more lasting consequence for philosophy and drawing us into the center of our historiographic question is that, by mid-century, a number of people in analytic philosophy were arguing that scientific philosophy was in an important sense a fundamentally confused project. Among the most forthright of these critics was Max Black, who had in the 1930s translated a number of Carnap's papers into English, for whom the rejection of scientific philosophy was an argument for Moore's version of analytic philosophy over Russell's. Here is how he puts the point in the introduction to his anthology of readings in philosophical analysis:

> By adopting the scientific method, philosophers are to learn from scientists and mathematicians how to agree; and steady calculation, guaranteed to produce an acceptable answer, is to replace philosophical disputation. If some such hope as this inspired Russell (as it certainly did the Logical Positivists, who learned so much from him) his program was a failure. The merits of his views on philosophical analysis have to be argued on *philosophical* grounds; and to baptize them as "scientific" can only generate confusion. (Black 1950, p. 6)

This kind of argument seems straightforwardly to beg the question against scientific philosophy. Carnap would ask here for both a specification of what sort of confusion is at stake and, more particularly, what "philosophical grounds" for metaphilosophical positions might be. But philosophy does not advance through the production of probative and non-question-begging arguments, but rather by finding enough reasons to set aside certain projects. For our purposes, Black provides us also with an argument by example that there were, in the mid-twentieth century, philosophers who were advocating for analytic philosophy who had not simply set aside the scientific ambitions of logical empiricism but indeed believed they had philosophical arguments that those ambitions could not be fulfilled.

Whatever else is true, material developments in American philosophy circa 1950 militated in favor of an analytic philosophy that went beyond the explicit scientific ambitions of the logical empiricists. There was a proliferation of anthologies of philosophical analysis and analytic philosophy published from about 1949 onward – the most famous of which, *Readings in Philosophical Analysis* (Feigl and Sellars 1949) was coedited by a member of the Vienna Circle, Herbert Feigl. Similarly, this time period saw the first production of journals and textbooks that had "analytic philosophy" in the title. All of these works explicitly or implicitly included logical empiricism within the purview of the project, but also included a fair range of other historical and contemporary projects. Why exactly this happened is not entirely clear – an explanatory history of such large-scale changes in philosophical framing has scarcely been on offer to this point for any such event in the history of philosophy. But it is clear that in the post–World War II era, a significant number of logical empiricists joined the Anglophone philosophical world, the vast majority heading to the USA, and they needed to find a place in a new philosophical world.

This institutional-cum-intellectual project – the need to find a place within the American philosophical world – seems most important for forging the new consensus on "analytic philosophy." The vast majority of their new American philosophical colleagues did not work in the kind of technical projects the logical empiricists were pursuing, and there were also several new colleagues from Britain who were deeply influenced by analytic but unscientific projects such as Moore's commonsense philosophy, Oxford ordinary language philosophy, and late Wittgenstein. Not drawing out commonalities but rather insisting on differences would be a radical and isolationist strategy for a new immigrant project, and it is clear that some logical empiricists (such as Feigl) explicitly and others (such as Carnap) more implicitly, chose the ecumenical and not isolationist route.

Broad-tent rhetoric is highly functional for a relatively powerless new project to gain a foothold in a new, potentially skeptical research community. It is not highly functional for advancing the specific goals of your own project as the only project that will bring appropriate intellectual standards to the doing of philosophy. In choosing the former, the logical empiricists made the latter much more difficult. Indeed, after Reichenbach's death in 1953, it is not clear that there was much of an effort to recruit many to the specifically scientific ambitions of the logical empiricist project.

A more curious phenomenon is one associated with some of the rhetoric of Quine's naturalist project. At various moments, Quine presents Carnap's *Aufbau* project as the last best hope for a traditional, nonscientific, foundationalist empiricism that, after Quine's rejection of the details of constructing the external world and his further rejection of the analytic/synthetic distinction, must be set aside in favor of a new, scientific empiricist naturalism. This metaphilosophical rhetoric was no doubt effective for more than a few readers, but it is surprising, for elsewhere Quine does show an understanding of the scientific ambitions of Carnap's project right back to the beginnings.

Our job in this Element has not been to unravel all mysteries or remake the philosophical universe. I will refrain from any effort to reach the final adjudication of this Carnap/Quine dispute here at the end. But the insistence on the scientific philosophy of logical empiricism does, again, sharpen issues. On the matter of Quine's naturalism more generally: Quine generally presented it as if was the inevitable consequence of the rejection of reductionism and the analytic/synthetic distinction. Carnap, however, thought it was more a presupposition of Quine's objections to the latter; Carnap saw Quine as demanding that he answer pragmatic, empirical questions about the analytic/synthetic distinction and Carnap rejected that such answers were necessary or pertinent to the philosophical burdens he placed on the distinction as a distinction within formal semantics. On Carnap's behalf, we might ask why philosophical engineering must justify its formal tools in ways other engineering projects do not.

My intention here is not to defend Carnapian logic of science. It would, however, be a shame if scientific philosophy were somehow limited to Quine's version of naturalism. First, it harms our ability to understand the history of philosophy in the nineteenth through twenty-first centuries. Second, it deprives us of tools for philosophical work here and now. Third, it restricts us to a form of scientific philosophy that in the view of many underemphasizes and misunderstands the use of formal tools in philosophy in general. The best way forward for the philosophical and historical consideration of logical empiricism now is not as a "back to logical empiricism" movement but rather as moving forward with a more nuanced and accurate understanding of what was at stake for the logical empiricists in their own work, taking from them what seems helpful to our own philosophical projects. It is our venture now.

References

Bergson, H. [1903] 1999. *Introduction to Metaphysics*. Indianapolis, IN: Hackett.

Black, M. 1950. Introduction. In M. Black (ed.), *Philosophical Analysis*, pp. 1–13. Englewood Cliffs, NJ: Prentice-Hall.

Blumberg, A. E. and H. Feigl. 1931. Logical Positivism. *Journal of Philosophy* 28(11): 281–296.

Brown, M. 2015. Politicizing Science: Conceptions of Politics in Science and Technology Studies. *Social Studies of Science* 45(1): 3–30.

Brun, G. 2016. Explication As a Method of Conceptual Re-engineering. *Erkenntnis* 81(6): 1211–1241.

Cappelen, H. 2018. *Fixing Language: An Essay on Conceptual Engineering*. Oxford: Oxford University Press.

Carnap, R. [1922] 2019b. Space: A Contribution to the Theory of Science. In P. W. Carus, M. Friedman, W. Kienzler, A. Richardson, and S. Schlotter (eds.), *The Collected Works of Rudolf Carnap, Volume 1: Early Writings*, pp. 21–171. Oxford: Oxford University Press.

Carnap, R. [1923] 2019a. On the Task of Physics and the Application of the Principle of Maximal Simplicity. In P. W. Carus, M. Friedman, W. Kienzler, A. Richardson, and S. Schlotter (eds.), *The Collected Works of Rudolf Carnap, Volume 1: Early Writings*, pp. 209–241. Oxford: Oxford University Press.

Carnap, R. [1928] 1961a. *The Logical Structure of the World*. Berkeley: University of California Press.

Carnap, R. [1928] 1961b. Pseudoproblems in Philosophy. In R. Carnap, *The Logical Structure of the World*, pp. 300–343. Berkeley: University of California Press.

Carnap, R. [1934] 1937. *The Logical Syntax of Language*. London: Kegan Paul, Trench, Trubner.

Carnap, R. 1935. *Philosophy and Logical Syntax*. London: Kegan Paul, Trench, Trubner.

Carnap, R. 1936/1937. Testability and Meaning. *Philosophy of Science* 3(4): 419–471; 4(1): 1–40.

Carnap, R. [1950] 1956a. Empiricism, Semantics, and Ontology. In R. Carnap, *Meaning and Necessity*. 2nd ed., pp. 205–221. Chicago, IL: University of Chicago Press.

Carnap, R. 1956b. *Meaning and Necessity.* 2nd ed. Chicago, IL: University of Chicago Press.

Carnap, R. 1963. Replies and Systematic Expositions. In P. A. Schilpp (ed.), *The Philosophy of Rudolf Carnap*, pp. 859–1013. LaSalle, IL: Open Court.

Cartwright, N., J. Cat, L. Fleck, and T. E. Uebel. 1996. *Otto Neurath: Philosophy between Science and Politics.* Cambridge: Cambridge University Press.

Carus, A. W. 2007. *Carnap and Twentieth-Century Thought.* Cambridge: Cambridge University Press.

Carus, A. W. 2016. Carnap and Phenomenology: What Happened in 1924? In C. Damböck (ed.), *Influences on the* Aufbau, pp. 137–162. Cham: Springer.

Carus, P. W., M. Friedman, W. Kienzler, A. Richardson, and S. Schlotter (eds.). 2019. *The Collected Works of Rudolf Carnap, Volume 1: Early Writings.* Oxford: Oxford University Press.

Cassirer, E. 1910. *Substanzbegriff und Functionsbegriff.* Berlin: B. Cassirer.

Cat, J. 2019. Neurath and the Legacy of Algebraic Logic. In J. Cat and A. Tuboly (eds.), *Neurath Reconsidered*, pp. 241–337. Cham: Springer.

Cat, J. and A. Tuboly (eds.). 2019. *Neurath Reconsidered.* Cham: Springer.

Creath, R. 1990. The Unimportance of Semantics. *Philosophy of Science Association* (1990): 405–416.

Creath, R. (ed.). 1991. *Dear Carnap, Dear Van.* Berkeley: University of California Press.

Damböck, C., G. Sander, and M. Werner (eds.). 2021. *Logical Empiricism, Life Reform, and the German Youth Movement.* Dordrecht: Springer.

Ducasse, C. J. 1941. *Philosophy As a Science.* New York: Oskar Piest.

Dutilh Novaes, C. 2020. Carnap Meets Foucault: Conceptual Engineering and Genealogical Investigations. *Inquiry.* https://doi.org/10.1080/0020174X.2020.1860122.

Edmonds, D. 2020. *The Murder of Professor Schlick.* Princeton, NJ: Princeton University Press.

Feigl, H. 1981. *Inquiries and Provocations.* Dordrecht: Reidel.

Feigl, Herbert, and Wilfrid Sellars (eds.). 1949. *Readings in Philosophical Analysis.* New York: Appleton-Century-Crofts.

Frank, P. [1946] 1955. *Foundations of Physics.* In O. Neurath, R. Carnap, and C. Morris (eds.), *The Encyclopedia of Unified Science, Volume 1*, pp. 423–504. Chicago, IL: University of Chicago Press.

Frank, P. 1951. *Modern Science and Its Philosophy.* Cambridge, MA: Harvard University Press.

Frege, G. [1884] 1960. *Foundations of Arithmetic.* Evanston, IL: Northwestern University Press.

Frege, G. [1893] 1997. *Grundgesetze der Arithmetik, Volume One*. Excerpts in M. Beaney (ed.), *The Frege Reader*, pp. 194–223. Oxford: Blackwell.

Friedman, J. T. and S. Luft (eds.). 2015. *The Philosophy of Ernst Cassirer*. Berlin: DeGruyter.

Friedman, M. 1983. *Foundations of Space-Time Theories*. Princeton, NJ: Princeton University Press.

Friedman, M. 1999. *Reconsidering Logical Positivism*. Cambridge: Cambridge University Press.

Friedman, M. 2000a. *A Parting of the Ways*. Chicago, IL: Open Court.

Friedman, M. 2000b. Hempel and the Vienna Circle. In J. H. Fetzer (ed.), *Science, Explanation, and Rationality*, pp. 39–64. Oxford: Oxford University Press.

Frost-Arnold, G. 2013. *Carnap, Tarski, and Quine at Harvard: Conversations on Logic, Mathematics, and Science*. Chicago, IL: Open Court.

Galison, P. 1996. Constructing Modernism: The Cultural Location of *Aufbau*. In R. N. Giere and A. Richardson (eds.), *Origins of Logical Empiricism*, pp. 17–44. Minneapolis: University of Minnesota Press.

Haller, R. 1993. *Neupositivismus*. Darmstadt: Wissenschaftliche Buchgesellschaft.

Harris, E. E. 1952. Scientific Philosophy. *Philosophical Quarterly* 2(7): 153–165.

Heidegger, M. [1925] 1985. *History of the Concept of Time*. Bloomington: Indiana University Press.

Heidegger, M. [1927] 1982. *Basic Problems of Phenomenology*. Bloomington: Indiana University Press.

Heidegger, M. [1928/1929] 1996. *Einleitung in die Philosophie*. Frankfurt: Vittorio Klostermann.

Heidegger, M. [1929] 1977. What Is Metaphysics? In M. Heidegger, *Basic Writings*, pp. 95–112. New York: Harper & Row.

Heis, J. 2010. "Critical Philosophy Begins at the Very Point Where Logistic Leaves Off": Cassirer's Response to Frege and Russell. *Perspectives on Science* 18(4): 383–408.

Hempel, C. G. 1965. *Aspects of Scientific Explanation*. New York: Free Press.

Hook, Sidney. 1930. A Personal Impression of Contemporary German Philosophy. *Journal of Philosophy* 27(6): 141–160.

Howard, D. 2003. Two Left Turns Make a Right: On the Curious Political Career of North American Philosophy of Science at Midcentury. In G. L. Hardcastle and A. Richardson (eds.), *Logical Empiricism in North America*, pp. 25–93. Minneapolis: University of Minnesota Press, 2003.

Howard, D. 2010. "Let Me Briefly Indicate Why I Do Not Find This Standpoint Natural": Einstein, General Relativity, and the Contingent a Priori. In

M. Domski and M. Dickson (eds.), *Discourse on a New Method*, pp. 333–355. LaSalle, IL: Open Court.

Husserl, E. [1911] 1965. Philosophy As Rigorous Science. In E. Husserl, *Phenomenology and the Crisis of Philosophy*, pp. 71–147. New York: Harper & Row.

Isaac, M. G., S. Koch, and R. Nedft. 2022. Conceptual Engineering: A Roadmap to Practice. *Philosophy Compass* 17(10): 1–15.

Joergensen, J. 1951. *The Development of Logical Empiricism*. Chicago, IL: University of Chicago Press.

Matherne, S. 2021. *Cassirer*. London: Routledge.

Merton, R. K. [1942] 1973. The Normative Structure of Science. In R. K. Merton, *The Sociology of Science*, pp. 267–278. Chicago, IL: University of Chicago Press.

Milkov, N. 2013. Carl Hempel: Whose Philosopher? In N. Milkov and V. Peckhaus (eds.), *The Berlin Group and the Philosophy of Logical Empiricism*, pp. 293–308. Dordrecht: Springer.

Milkov, N. and V. Peckhaus (eds.). 2013. *The Berlin Group and the Philosophy of Logical Empiricism*. Dordrecht: Springer.

Morris, C. 1935. Science of Philosophy and Philosophy of Science. *Philosophy of Science* 2(3): 271–286.

Nagel, E. 1936. Impressions and Appraisals of Analytic Philosophy in Europe. I. *Journal of Philosophy* 33(1): 5–24.

Nemeth, E. 1981. *Otto Neurath und der Wiener Kreis*. Frankfurt: Campus.

Neurath, O. [1938] 1955. Unified Science As Encyclopedic Integration. In O. Neurath, R. Carnap, and C. Morris (eds.), *The Encyclopedia of Unified Science, Volume 1*, pp. 1–27. Chicago, IL: University of Chicago Press.

Neurath, O. 1983. *Philosophical Papers, 1913–1946*. Dordrecht: Reidel.

Neurath, O, R. Carnap, and H. Hahn. [1929] 2012. *Wissenschaftliche Weltauffassung. Der Wiener Kreis*. Reprint and translation ed. F. Stadler and T. E. Uebel (eds.). Vienna: Springer.

Padovani, F. 2011. Relativizing the Relativized a Priori: Reichenbach's Axioms of Coordination Divided. *Synthese* 181(1): 41–62.

Padovani, F. 2021. Hans Reichenbach and the Freistudentenschaft: School Reform, Pedagogy, and Freedom. In C. Damböck et al. (eds.), *Logical Empiricism, Life Reform, and the German Youth Movement*, pp. 81–103. Dordrecht: Springer.

Passmore, J. 1957. *A Hundred Years of Philosophy*. London: Duckworth.

Poincaré, H. [1902] 2017. *Science and Hypothesis*. London: Bloomsbury.

Popper, K. R. [1963] 2002. *Conjectures and Refutations*. London: Routledge.

Putnam, R. A. 1978. UCLA, 1951–53. In H. Reichenbach, *Selected Writings, 1909–1953, Volume One*, pp. 61–64. Dordrecht: Reidel.

Quine, W. V. 1951. Two Dogmas of Empiricism. *Philosophical Review* 60(1): 20–43.

Quine, W.V. 1960. *Word and Object*. Cambridge, MA: MIT Press.

Quine, W. V. 1963. Carnap and Logical Truth. In P. A. Schilpp (ed.), *The Philosophy of Rudolf Carnap*, pp. 385–406. LaSalle, IL: Open Court.

Quine, W. V. 1969. Epistemology Naturalized. In W. V. Quine, *Ontological Relativity and Other Essays*, pp. 69–90. New York. Columbia University Press.

Quine, W. V. 1981. Five Milestones of Empiricism. In W. V. Quine, *Theories and Things*, pp. 67–72. Cambridge, MA: Harvard Belknap.

Reichenbach, H. [1913] 1978. The Free Student Idea: Its Unified Contents. In H. Richenbach, *Selected Writings, 1909–1953, Volume One*, pp. 108–123. Dordrecht: Reidel.

Reichenbach, H. [1916] 2008. *The Concept of Probability in the Mathematical Representation of Reality*. LaSalle, IL: Open Court.

Reichenbach, H. [1920] 1965. *The Theory of Relativity and a Priori Knowledge*. Berkeley: University of California Press.

Reichenbach, H. [1928] 1958. *The Philosophy of Space and Time*. New York: Dover.

Reichenbach, H. [1929] 1978. New Approaches in Science: Philosophical Research. In H. Reichenbach, *Selected Writings, 1909–1953, Volume One*, pp. 249–253. Dordrecht: Reidel.

Reichenbach, H. [1930] 1978. The Philosophical Significance of Modern Physics. In H. Reichenbach, *Selected Writings, 1909–1953, Volume One*, pp. 304–323. Dordrecht: Reidel.

Reichenbach, H. 1936. Logistic Empiricism and the Current State of Its Problems. *Journal of Philosophy* 33(6): 141–160.

Reichenbach, H. 1951. *The Rise of Scientific Philosophy*. Berkeley: University of California Press.

Reichenbach, H. 1978. *Selected Writings, 1909–1953, Volume One*. Dordrecht: Reidel.

Reisch, G. 2005. *How the Cold War Transformed Philosophy of Science*. Cambridge: Cambridge University Press.

Richardson, A. 1997. Toward a History of Scientific Philosophy. *Perspectives on Science* 5(3): 418–451.

Richardson, A. 1998. *Carnap's Construction of the World*. Cambridge: Cambridge University Press.

Richardson, A. 2013. Taking the Measure of Carnap's Philosophical Engineering: Metalogic As Metrology. In E. Reck (ed.), *The Historical Turn in Analytic Philosophy*, pp. 60–77. Basingstoke: Palgrave MacMillan.

Richardson, A. 2016. Cassirer's *Substance Concept and Functional Concept*. In E. Schliesser (ed.), *Ten Neglected Classics of Philosophy*, pp. 177–194. Oxford: Oxford University Press.

Richardson, A. 2017. "Neither a Confession nor an Accusation": Michael Polanyi, Hans Reichenbach, and Philosophical Modernity after World War One. *Historical Studies in the Natural Sciences* 47 (2017): 423–442.

Richardson, A. 2021. Hans Reichenbach, Radio Philosopher. *Synthese* 199(5/6): 12625–12641.

Richardson, S. 2009a. The Left Vienna Circle, Part 1. Carnap, Neurath, and the Left Vienna Circle Thesis. *Studies in History and Philosophy of Science* 40(1): 14–24.

Richardson, S. 2009b. The Left Vienna Circle, Part 2. The Left Vienna Circle, Disciplinary History, and Feminist Philosophy of Science. *Studies in History and Philosophy of Science* 40(2): 167–174.

Ringer, F. 1969. *The Decline of the German Mandarins: The German Academic Community, 1890–1933*. Cambridge, MA: Harvard University Press.

Romizi, D. 2012. The Vienna Circle's "Scientific World-Conception": Philosophy of Science in the Political Arena. *HOPOS: Journal of the International Society for the History of Philosophy of Science* 2(2): 205–242.

Russell, Bertrand. [1914] 1993. *Our Knowledge of the External World*. London: Routledge.

Ryckman, T. 2005. *The Reign of Relativity*. Oxford: Oxford University Press.

Ryckman, T. 2008. Carnap and Husserl. In M. Friedman and R. Creath (eds.), *The Cambridge Companion to Carnap*, pp. 81–105. Cambridge: Cambridge University Press.

Sarkar, S. 2003. Husserl's Role in Carnap's *Der Raum*. In T. Bonk (ed.), *Language, Truth, and Knowledge*, pp. 179–190. Dordrecht: Kluwer.

Scheler, M. [1913] 2018. *Versuche einer Philosophie des Lebens*. Munich: Albunea.

Schlick, M. [1918/1925] 1974. *General Theory of Knowledge*. Vienna: Springer.

Schlick, M. [1919] 1963. *Space and Time in Contemporary Physics*. New York: Dover.

Schlick, M. [1930] 1959. The Turning Point in Philosophy. In A. J. Ayer (ed.), *Logical Positivism*, pp. 53–59. New York: Free Press.

Soames, S. 2018. *The Analytic Tradition in Philosophy, Volume 2: A New Vision*. Princeton, NJ: Princeton University Press.

Spengler, O. [1918/1922] 1991.*The Decline of the West*. Oxford: Oxford University Press.

Stadler, F. 2015. *The Vienna Circle*. 2nd ed. Vienna: Springer.

Stone, A. 2006. Heidegger and Carnap on the Overcoming of Metaphysics. In S. Mulhall (ed.), *Martin Heidegger*, pp. 217–244. London: Routledge.

Stroll, A. 2001. *Twentieth-Century Analytic Philosophy*. New York: Columbia University Press.

Uebel, T. E. 2004. Education, Enlightenment, and Positivism: The Vienna Circle's *Scientific World-Conception* Revisited. *Science & Education* 13(1/2): 41–66.

Uebel, T. E. 2005. Political Philosophy of Science in Logical Empiricism: The Left Vienna Circle. *Studies in History and Philosophy of Science* 36(4): 754–773.

Uebel, T. E. 2010. What's Right about Carnap, Neurath and the Left Vienna Circle Thesis: A Refutation. *Studies in History and Philosophy of Science* 41(2): 214–221.

Uebel, T. E. 2012. On the Production History and Early Reception of *The Scientific Conception of the World. The Vienna Circle*. In O. Neurath et al., *Wissenschaftliche Weltauffassung. Der Wiener Kreis*. Reprint and translation ed. F. Stadler and T. E. Uebel (eds.), pp. 291–314. Vienna: Springer.

Uebel, T. E. 2015. *Empiricism at the Crossroads*. LaSalle, IL: Open Court.

Uebel, T. E. 2020. Intersubjective Accountability: Politics and Philosophy in the Left Vienna Circle. *Perspectives on Science* 28(1): 35–62.

Verhaegh, S. 2020. The American Reception of Logical Positivism: First Encounters (1929–1932). *HOPOS: Journal of the International Society for the History of Philosophy of Science* 10(1): 106–142.

Wittgenstein, L. [1921] 2001. *Tractatus Logico-Philosophicus*. London: Routledge.

Acknowledgments

This Element summarizes a portion of a research program I have pursued for a quarter century. I thank Jacob Stegenga for the invitation to write it and two anonymous reviewers for comments on the manuscript. The number of people whose work and interest has advanced this research program is far too high to thank them individually. My work on logical empiricism has been most inspired and informed by the work of Michael Friedman, Thomas E. Uebel, and Friedrich Stadler; I owe them a debt of gratitude that cannot be repaid. Generations of students at the University of British Columbia have helped me sort through this material and I thank them all. During the drafting of material I have drawn on for this Element, I was aided by research assistance provided by Dani Inkpen and Vlada Asadulaeva that was funded by the Social Sciences and Humanities Research Council of Canada and the University of British Columbia Public Humanities Hub.

For Judy Z. Segal, the best person and the best professor I know

Philosophy of Science

Jacob Stegenga
University of Cambridge

Jacob Stegenga is a Reader in the Department of History and Philosophy of Science at the University of Cambridge. He has published widely on fundamental topics in reasoning and rationality and philosophical problems in medicine and biology. Prior to joining Cambridge he taught in the United States and Canada, and he received his PhD from the University of California San Diego.

About the Series

This series of Elements in Philosophy of Science provides an extensive overview of the themes, topics and debates which constitute the philosophy of science. Distinguished specialists provide an up-to-date summary of the results of current research on their topics, as well as offering their own take on those topics and drawing original conclusions.

Cambridge Elements ≡

Philosophy of Science

Elements in the Series

Duhem and Holism
Milena Ivanova

Bayesianism and Scientific Reasoning
Jonah N. Schupbach

Fundamentality and Grounding
Kerry McKenzie

Values in Science
Kevin C. Elliott

Scientific Representation
James Nguyen and Roman Frigg

Philosophy of Open Science
Sabina Leonelli

Natural Kinds
Muhammad Ali Khalidi

Scientific Progress
Darrell P. Rowbottom

Modelling Scientific Communities
Cailin O'Connor

Science and the Public
Angela Potochnik

Logical Empiricism as Scientific Philosophy
Alan Richardson

A full series listing is available at: www.cambridge.org/EPSC

Printed in the United States
by Baker & Taylor Publisher Services